MW01089415

The Fall of Heaven

by Walter Mosley

SAMUEL FRENCH

FOUNDED 1830

NEW YORK HOLLYWOOD LONDON TORONTO

SAMUELFRENCH.COM

ISBN 978-0-573-60105-7   Printed in U.S.A.   #29765

MUSIC USE NOTE

Licensees are solely responsible for obtaining formal written permission from copyright owners to use copyrighted music in the performance of this play and are strongly cautioned to do so. If no such permission is obtained by the licensee, then the licensee must use only original music that the licensee owns and controls. Licensees are solely responsible and liable for all music clearances and shall indemnify the copyright owners of the play and their licensing agent, Samuel French, Inc., against any costs, expenses, losses and liabilities arising from the use of music by licensees.

IMPORTANT BILLING AND CREDIT
REQUIREMENTS

All producers of *THE FALL OF HEAVEN must* give credit to the Author of the Play in all programs distributed in connection with performances of the Play, and in all instances in which the title of the Play appears for the purposes of advertising, publicizing or otherwise exploiting the Play and/ or a production. The name of the Author *must* appear on a separate line on which no other name appears, immediately following the title and *must* appear in size of type not less than fifty percent of the size of the title type.

In addition the following credit *must* be given in all programs and publicity information distributed in association with this piece:

THE FALL OF HEAVEN
By Walter Mosley
Based on the novel "The Tempest Tales" by Walter Mosley

THE FALL OF HEAVEN was originally produced by Cincinatti Playhouse in the Park (Edward Stern, Producing Artistic Director; Buzz Ward, Executive Director), at the Robert S. Marx Theatre in Cincinatti, Ohio on January 23, 2010. The performance was directed by Marion McClinton, with sets by David Gallo, costumes by Karen Perry, lighting by Donald Holder, sound by Rob Millburn and Michael Bodeen, fight direction by Drew Fracher. The production stage manager was Jennifer Morrow. The cast was as follows:

TEMPEST LANDRY . . . . .Leland Gantt

JOSHUA ANGEL/MAN #1 . . . . Esau Pritchett

BASIL BOB/SAINT PETER/
      MAN #2/OFFSTAGE VOICES . . . . Anthony Marble

BRANWYN WEEKS/WOMAN #2 . . . . .Heather Alicia Simms

ALFREDA/DARLENE/WOMAN #1 . . . . .Joy C. Hooper

NEW YORKERS/OTHERS. . . . . Lily Blau, Kristen B. Johnson,
Anthony Vaughn Merchant, Jacqueline Raposo
and Joe Watts, Jr.

CHARACTERS

Man 1 - **TEMPEST LANDRY** - African American, handsome, 30s

Man 2 - **JOSHUA ANGEL** - African American, approximately the same age as Tempest

Man 3 - **BOB** - White, 30s, dashing, all other male roles

Woman 1 - **BRANWYN** - African American, late 20s/early 30s, naturally attractive

Woman 2 - **ALFREDA** - African American, all other female roles, approximately the same age as Branwyn

A NOTE ON THE CASTING

The original production of *The Fall of Heaven* used 5 main actors (3 men and 2 woman) to portray all principal roles and 5 actors (3 woman and 2 men) to play Extras, ensemble roles. The breakdown for doubling was as follows:

TEMPEST LANDRY

JOSHUA ANGEL/MAN #1

BASIL BOB/SAINT PETER/MAN #2/OFFSTAGE VOICES

BRANWYN WEEKS/WOMAN #2

ALFREDA/DARLENE/WOMAN #1

NEW YORKERS/OTHERS

ACT ONE

Scene One

(Commercial Harlem street in the afternoon. Sounds of traffic and a far off police siren can be heard. A **PEDESTRIAN***, enters stage. He's walking slowly, his face hidden by the newspaper he's reading.)*

(Enter **WOMAN***, her back is nearly fully turned toward audience.)*

WOMAN. Clarence. Clarence!

(The woman hurries over to engage the man. They begin to talk. They turn and walk together exiting.)

(Enter **TEMPEST LANDRY***. He's talking – the cellphone in one hand and an MP3 player, earphones dangling, in the other.)*

(Tempest is a handsome man in his 30s, with neatly braided cornrows going down the back of his neck. He's wearing tan slacks and a dark, square cut shirt.)

TEMPEST. …Alfreda, Al Baby, how does this damn thing you give me work?…No. It gets to the middle of a Roberta Flack song and then it go back to the beginnin' or to a whole 'nother song…No, I'm doin' it right. It's just… Hold up.

(checks phone)

(The sirens are getting louder.)

It's my wife. Don't hang up. I'ma put you on hold.

(presses button to switch call)

TEMPEST. *(cont.)* Hey, Baby. What's up?…No…No…I'm on my way home. I bought this new MP3 player for ya… No, I didn't spend the money for your blood pressure medicine….

(A black **MAN** *dressed somewhat like* **TEMPEST** *races at full speed across the stage.)*

What the fuck?…I gotta go, Linda…What? No. I ain't talkin' to no Alfreda Robins. See you in ten minutes. Bye.

(He presses a button to talk.)

(Sirens get louder still.)

Alfreda, you still there? Hey, Baby. I love you but this a piece'a junk you give me…

*(***TEMPEST** *holds the MP3 player up, nothing like a pistol.)*

VOICE. *(offstage)* He's got a gun!

(Shots ring out. **TEMPEST** *is hit multiple times. Blood, phone, and MP3 go flying, and he falls to the ground, obviously dead. The lights lower and sirens slowly merge into a souful tune, something like "Killing Me Softly" sung by Roberta Flack.*)*

(blackout)

---

* Please see Music Use Note on Page 3.

Scene Two

(Soft celestial music begins playing. Lights come up on an eerie and ethereal backdrop of blues and grays that are reminiscent of the sky. The stage might be in that sky.)

(A long line of dead souls – covered from head to toe in gray, white, black, and ochre robes – is moving across the stage slowly, without anyone taking a step. Amid these dead souls is **TEMPEST LANDRY** *wearing the same clothes he was shot down in.)*

(At one side of the stage, seated behind a huge stone slab which he uses as a desk, is bearded, white **SAINT PETER.***)*

(To Peter's left is a portal lit from within by golden light. To his right is a portal that is dark and forboding.)

*(***PETER** *is addressing these souls one by one, listing their transgressions.)*

SAINT PETER. You stole your brother's savings jar from your dead mother's home.

(The hooded **PENITENT** *nods.)*

You stole from your employers, lied to your wife, beat your children out of anger without concern or restraint.

PENITENT. I know, I know.

(Judge and the accused regard each other. **PETER** *makes a gesture toward the portal to Hell. The* **PENITENT** *groans even as he makes his way toward eternal damnation.)*

*(***TEMPEST** *addresses the hooded figure in front of him.)*

TEMPEST. That one was pretty cut and dry. Don't you think?

(There is no response so he turns to the person behind.)

Not like that one they had a long time ago – you remember, the one where the woman had murdered her sister for usin' her own perfume while committin' adultery with her husband...

(With no response from the figure directly behind **TEMPEST** *steps out of line far enough to address the soul two places back.)*

TEMPEST. *(cont.)* I mean the woman probably used her sister's perfume to save her from smellin' another woman's scent on her man.

(back to the one in front of him)

You think the murdered sister got sent below too? Prob'ly she did. Prob'ly so.

*(***TEMPEST** *is the next in line, but he isn't paying attention.)*

Damn. I been on this line seem like forever. I spent more time with you guys than I have with my own kids and not one'a you says a damn word. I cain't tell if you man or woman in them robes. You know you could say sumpin'. I mean listenin' to all those private sins and judgements… well, I don't know…it just don't seem right.

(The last soul before **TEMPEST** *has trundled off to Hell.)*

SAINT PETER. Tempest Landry!

TEMPEST. Finally!

*(***TEMPEST** *turns around and approaches the highest judge.* **PETER** *frowns and tries to stare* **TEMPEST** *down but the confirmed Harlemite is unaffected.)*

Let's get on with it, huh? You know I got some friends bet me I wouldn'ta evah make it this far.

*(***PETER** *turns back to his book, looks for the page and begins reading.)*

SAINT PETER. You stabbed Quinten Sams on July third when you were only fifteen years old…

*(***PETER** *is about to go on but* **TEMPEST** *interrupts.)*

TEMPEST. Excuse me, your honor, but that there was self-defense. Q-boy was reachin' for a pistol in his pocket when he saw me kissin' on a girl forgot to tell him that she had broke it off with him earlier that mornin'. And I only stuck him in the arm.

SAINT PETER. This is not a discussion, boy. This is your final judgement. The sins have been gathered by Joshua, the accounting angel of Heaven. There is no defense…

TEMPEST. *Boy?*

SAINT PETER. At seventeen you stole three hundred fourteen dollars and seventy-nine cents from your mother's own church…

TEMPEST. Stole? No. I only *took* from Reverend Langly's collection box. I mean I seen him throwin' away the congregation's money on women and drug down at Bertha Burnett's ho'house. I used that money to pay for my auntie's groceries while she was recoverin' from the pneumonia. The way I see it, I was takin' the church's money away from the Devil and puttin' it to work the way it was meant to be used.

*(***PETER** *slams the book shut, rises to his feet, and uses his Celestial Voice {mic'd} to address* **TEMPEST**.*)*

SAINT PETER. Your lies helped to convict Tiny Henderson of a crime which he did not commit…

*(***TEMPEST** *is momentarily stunned by the booming voice but he recovers.)*

TEMPEST. Now, Judge, I admit that there's some gray area in these other accusations. But in the case of Tiny Henderson versus Harlem-in-general, I think you have to agree that it was my duty to bear false witness against that neighbor.

SAINT PETER. Your duty?

TEMPEST. Yeah. Tiny had raped, brutalized, and murdered throughout our community and had not been convicted or even arrested for years. I knew a man he killed. I heard him brag on it. So when I lied it was really a truth. It's just that Tiny hadn't done the one thing but he had another.

(The Celestial Music turns into the murmuring of thousands of **ANGELS** *concerned about the turn of this judgement.)*

(PETER's begins to rise and his rage becomes a tower before his nemesis. TEMPEST falls back a step staring up at the divine judge.)

SAINT PETER. Go to Hell!

(TEMPEST looks up at the judge and then over at the dark portal. He looks up again and slowly shakes his head.)

TEMPEST. No.

(The murmuring ceases and silence reigns.)

SAINT PETER. No?

TEMPEST. You said what you think I did wrong, and I give you my reasons why. But you didn't come back and say why my whys was wrong.

SAINT PETER. You refuse celestial judgement?

TEMPEST. If that's what you call it. Yeah.

SAINT PETER. No one can refuse the judgement of Heaven. Sinner or saint, rich man or pauper – they all bow their heads to me…

TEMPEST. I don't know about all that. All I can tell you is I ain't goin' unless you prove to me that I done wrong. Either that or you throw me in the pit yourself.

(PETER stares, the rage mounting in him.)

(PETER shouts in his Celestial Voice. TEMPEST cowers but he does not go toward Hell.)

(PETER raises his hands to the Heavens and brings them down with great force.)

(thunderous SFX)

(blackout)

Scene Three

(Lights come up on the Harlem street scene again.
TEMPEST*'s cornrows are gone. His hair is now natural and longish.* **TEMPEST** *is standing on the corner shocked, disoriented. He feels for the bullet holes.)*

(Unnoticed, **JOSHUA ANGEL** *is watching the confused soul.)*

*(***ANGEL** *is a black man approximately the same age as Tempest. He's wearing a very nice light colored suit.)*

(A **WOMAN** *is walking by.)*

TEMPEST. Excuse me, Ma'am.

WOMAN. Yes?

TEMPEST. Was there gunfire around here a few minutes ago?

WOMAN. No, not a few minutes ago. Two, three years ago the police shot down an innocent man right where you're standing. Shot him seventeen times. They had a protest march and everything but he's still dead.

TEMPEST. Dead? What was his name?

WOMAN. I don't remember.

TEMPEST. Tell me his name. Think.

*(***TEMPEST** *grabs her arm and she pulls away.)*

WOMAN. Get your hands off me, man.

TEMPEST. But…

(The **WOMAN** *hurries off.* **TEMPEST** *is greatly disturbed. As he looks around* **JOSHUA** *slowly approaches.)*

JOSHUA. Excuse me. Mr. Landry?

TEMPEST. Who are you?

JOSHUA. Welcome back to Earth.

TEMPEST. Back? You mean that wasn't no dream?

(The **ANGEL** *shakes his head in agreement.)*

I died? No.

JOSHUA. Look in the glass.

TEMPEST. What you talkin' 'bout, man?

JOSHUA. Look in the glass.

(**TEMPEST** *goes to the window in a nearby building and looks at his reflection in the glass. He falls back in horror.*)

TEMPEST. What happened to my face?

JOSHUA. The Infinite has thrown you back, Tempest. They've given you a new body and sent me along to monitor your progress.

TEMPEST. Progress? What progress?

JOSHUA. I was sent to help you reexamine the circumstances of your life. When you agree that the judgement against you was valid you will enter immediately into Hell.

TEMPEST. You mean that really was Peter…judging me?

JOSHUA. You have been sentenced to Hell.

TEMPEST. But I got a chance if I, I…

JOSHUA. A reprieve…but only if you agree to enter a conversation with me concerning the disposition of your immortal soul.

TEMPEST. And if I don't agree?

(*The* **ANGEL** *might be about to say something but does not. This concept of disagreement with the Infinite is foreign.*)

JOSHUA. Do you accept this proposal?

TEMPEST. What if I don't?

JOSHUA. You can go back to the end of the line and start over.

TEMPEST. That many more years?…Tell me sumpin', brother. Are you a black man or just a white man made up to look like he was black?

JOSHUA. I am an angel. Not black or white, not man at all. Angels came before mankind.

TEMPEST. I died?

(JOSHUA *nods.*)

But because I said no to Hell I'm alive again in another man's body?

(JOSHUA *nods.*)

And you ain't no white man?

(JOSHUA *shakes his head.*)

TEMPEST. But if I say no to this...this what you call it?

JOSHUA. A conversation on the nature of your sins.

TEMPEST. So-called sins.

(JOSHUA *shrugs.*)

(**TEMPEST** *takes a moment to consider, then he nods.*)

An', an', an' if I refuse to play your game I gotta get back on line with the hundreds'a miles of deaf mutes in bathrobes?

(*The* **ANGEL** *makes a noncommittal gesture.*)

How much time I got to decide?

JOSHUA. The time is now.

(**TEMPEST** *takes a moment to consider.*)

TEMPEST. Okay. A'ight. Yeah. Okay. I'll give it a go. Either you prove to me that I'm a sinner or I prove to you that there's more to me than you know.

(*The* **ANGEL** *holds out a hand.* **TEMPEST** *hesitates and then shakes the proffered hand.*)

JOSHUA. Call me Joshua, Joshua Angel. You must be a little confused after all that's happened. Why don't you take a week to get reoriented? Let's say that we meet again in a week's time, next Tuesday at noon at that bar across the street.

(*The handshake goes on for a beat too long. They let go. The* **ANGEL** *seems supremely confident.* **TEMPEST** *is calculating, maybe a bit fearful.*)

TEMPEST. Okay, then. I'll see you a week from today, at noon. What's the date anyway?

JOSHUA. July 23, two thousand nine.

TEMPEST. I really been dead three years?

JOSHUA. See you in a week, Tempest.

(The **ANGEL** *turns and walks away.* **TEMPEST** *watches him until he exits. He waits a beat and then hurries off in the opposite direction.)*

(transition to:)

Scene Four

(*Lights come up on the interior of Reno's Bar and Restaurant.* **JOSHUA ANGEL** *is sitting at a small table. He's looking up now and again, checking his watch. The* **ANGEL** *is disturbed. He picks up the bill, takes money from his wallet and puts it in the sleeve. Looking around one more time he stands up.*)

(*Just then* **TEMPEST** *storms in. Somewhat disheveled he's dressed as he has been since being shot down three years before. He approaches* **JOSHUA** *angrily.*)

TEMPEST. Where the Hell have you been?

JOSHUA. I'm not the one who's late, Mr. Landry. Please, have a seat.

(**TEMPEST** *is irate but finally sits.* **JOSHUA** *follows suit.*)

TEMPEST. I been out on that corner every day lookin' for you, Angel.

JOSHUA. I don't understand. We agreed to meet today didn't we?

TEMPEST. I agreed to that before I looked in my pocket and found it empty. My girlfriend, Alfreda, had given me a hundred dollars to pay for my wife's blood pressure medication.

JOSHUA. Your girlfriend was paying for your wife's medication?

TEMPEST. Yeah. Otherwise I'da had to work overtime and we couldn't see each other. But when I looked there wasn't no money whatsoever in my pocket. I had all my same clothes, even the same holes in my socks, but the money was gone. Now why anybody from Heaven wanna pick my pocket?

JOSHUA. It's all part of the test.

TEMPEST. What test? I didn't agree to take no test.

JOSHUA. Your resurrection is meant for you to reexamine your sins.

TEMPEST. So-called sins.

JOSHUA. And what did you do when you found that you had no money?

TEMPEST. After you picked my pocket you mean. I was in a Duane Reade drug store tryin' to get me some aspirin 'cause it still hurt where I was shot.

JOSHUA. Yes. Your body is new and whole but your soul still recalls the accidental shooting.

TEMPEST. Now there you go lyin'. Them cops shootin' me wasn't no accident. You don't take no scared white boys cain't tell the difference between one black man and another, give 'em guns, let 'em run around the streets of Harlem and then say it's a accident one day when they shoot down a innocent man. Was it a accident that time they arrested me and beat me tryin' to get a confession for a robbery I didn't commit? No sir. The accident was me bein' a black man out in the open.

JOSHUA. I only meant to say that your mind remembered the pain of your death. That's why you needed the painkiller.

TEMPEST. Only I couldn't get it 'cause the Infinite stoled my money.

JOSHUA. An honest man, when he finds himself broke, looks for a job.

TEMPEST. Are you sure you ain't a white man under that black face, brother?

JOSHUA. Race means no more to me than it does to the stars.

TEMPEST. That must be true because in this day and age even a white man knows that you cain't get a job without a phone number and you can't get that without a place to send the bills at, and at least a few dollahs.

JOSHUA. I never considered that. When I applied for my job I already had a place to send the mail, and a phone.

TEMPEST. You got a job?

JOSHUA. Of course. I have to survive as a mortal while we inquire into your sins.

TEMPEST. So-called sins.

(The ANGEL *acquiesces with a gesture.)*

So you got a job and an apartment just like everybody else?

JOSHUA. How else would I survive?

TEMPEST. I'ont know. I guess I figured that you went back up to heaven every night after checking on us restless souls.

JOSHUA. You are my only charge, Mr. Landry. The Infinite has made me into a mortal man. Except for a quirk in my vocals chords I am as human as you.

TEMPEST. Even still, how can you judge me when you got it so easy that you cain't know how I feel?

(The next bit of dialogue transitions into JOSHUA*'s Celestial Voice as the speech goes on.)*

JOSHUA. I have aeons of experience with human suffering, Mr. Landry. I saw Moses rise up against the pharaohs, Attila the Hun rage across Europe. I've stood with the dying in the gas chambers at Treblinka and watched as African women sank in the cold Atlantic with their babies in their arms.

TEMPEST. Yeah, yeah. But have you evah been hungry?

JOSHUA. Excuse me?

TEMPEST. Have you ever bled or hurt or went without? Have you ever lost someone you loved?

(The ANGEL *again seems to want to respond but cannot.)*

I went to my mother's house Wednesday last but she didn't know me. She gave me that look she got for bill collectors and door to door bible thumpers. How would you know what that felt like? To have your own mother look at you like you was dog shit on the sidewalk?

JOSHUA. We're not here to question my understanding. It is you who has to understand.

TEMPEST. And I think it's you... Bartender. Gimme a sour mash double shot and put it on his bill.

(The **ANGEL** *adds money to what he's already left.)*

JOSHUA. Enjoy your drink. But I have to go. Very tired.

TEMPEST. Angels get tired?

JOSHUA. I've been working hard at my job. As long as I'm here I'm as mortal as any other man or woman. And it's so different here.

TEMPEST. Different how?

JOSHUA. In heaven there is no such thing as time passing. We have eternity to do whatever it is that we want. Here I work twelve hours a day just to do what they expect in eight.

TEMPEST. That ain't nuthin'. Poor man struggle twenty-four seven an' he still movin' backwards.

*(***JOSHUA*** sighs heavily.)*

JOSHUA. Do you need the money for rent?

TEMPEST. Naw. I got me a place just last night.

JOSHUA. How did you manage that? You said that your mother turned you away.

TEMPEST. My wife too. None'a my friends would talk to me neither. So I lifted a United Charities Fund donation box at Hildebrandt department store down on Thirty-fourth Street.

JOSHUA. You stole?

TEMPEST. Not the way I see it. Contribution box is for charity. Charity is for the poor. And I'm just about the poorest man you could meet. No money. No family. No friends. I bought me some watches from a guy who sells these knockoffs wholesale and sold 'em in the street till I had enough to get me a room.

JOSHUA. But you stole.

TEMPEST. And that was wrong. But I put the money back after I used it for what it was meant for. You know that forty-seven dollars an' fourty-four cent would'a been shaved down to just a few bucks aftah the charity took their piece. I just cut out the middle man.

JOSHUA. But you admit that you were wrong.

TEMPEST. Not so wrong that I deserve Hell.

(The **ANGEL** *sighs and sits back. The discussion weighs on him whereas* **TEMPEST** *seems to be invigorated by the interaction.)*

JOSHUA. Your logic is wrong. I'm sure of it. But I'm too tired to argue. Let's get together Saturday, at three P.M., at the reading room of the library on Forty-second Street. I'll be awake and able to debate you then.

*(***JOSHUA** *stands and sighs.)*

TEMPEST. Not so easy when you an' the so-called sinner standin' toe to toe is it?

(The angel shakes his head in disgust and turns away. **TEMPEST** *calls out tothe bartender.)*

Where my whiskey at?

Scene Five

*(Reading room of the New York Public Library. Off in a corner are three tables. A hippie-looking **WHITE GUY**, a **BLACK WOMAN** with red dreadlocks, and **TEMPEST** are all sitting at the same table. While the other two are reading, **TEMPEST** is building a pyramidal structure from a deck of playing cards. He's just now placing the last triangle at the top of the structure. He's concentrating, using a very light touch.)*

*(**JOSHUA ANGEL** walks in and a breeze knocks over **TEMPEST**'s transient work of art.)*

TEMPEST. Damn.

WOMAN. Shh!

*(**TEMPEST** doesn't like being shushed.)*

*(The **ANGEL** walks up to **TEMPEST** and takes the seat next to him.)*

TEMPEST. You walk in the room an' everything I done gets knocked over.

JOSHUA. How are you, Tempest?

TEMPEST. If I say fine do I go to hell? Or if I say, not so good today, do a trapdoor open up under my chair?

JOSHUA. I'm not here to trick you.

TEMPEST. No? Then tell me somethin'. You know my record. Do you think I'm such a bad sinner that I deserve eternal damnation?

JOSHUA. That was Peter's decree.

TEMPEST. I ain't askin' him.

JOSHUA. It is the judgement of heaven that you have used your free will in vain... that you are, are...

TEMPEST. Are what?

WOMAN. Shh!

TEMPEST. What the hell?

JOSHUA. Come on, Tempest. These people are trying to read. Let's go to that table over there.

(TEMPEST still doesn't like being shushed. The *WOMAN* doesn't like being interrupted. *ANGEL* leads *TEMPEST* away by the arm and gets him settled at a nearby vacant table.)

TEMPEST. Okay, so how is this supposed to work?

JOSHUA. I'm not really sure. This situation is unique. No one has ever refused the decree of heaven. Between you and I, no one suspected that human free will went so far.

TEMPEST. So you cain't send me to hell unless I say okay?

JOSHUA. That's right.

TEMPEST. It don't sound right to me.

JOSHUA. What don't you understand?

TEMPEST. I understand everything. It just stinks that's all.

JOSHUA. You aren't making any sense.

TEMPEST. I must be makin' some kinda sense, Angel. I must be makin' some kinda sense otherwise you'd be back up in the choir and I'd be cookin' on Satan's spit.

JOSHUA. This kind of talk, this human relativism, will get usnowhere.

TEMPEST. I don't know what the 'R' word means but I understand nowhere. Nowhere was where I went after them cops murdered me.

JOSHUA. You were not murdered. The men who killed you were upholding the law.

TEMPEST. Law? Did they kill me?

JOSHUA. Yes, but-

TEMPEST. Did I do anything that they should kill me for?

JOSHUA. No, however-

TEMPEST. Did they mean to kill me?

JOSHUA. Not specifically, they were worried about-

TEMPEST. Listen. Four men kill another man - an unarmed, innocent man. That's murder in my book.

JOSHUA. You were making some other point I believe.

TEMPEST. Yeah... uh...

*(**TEMPEST** has lost the thread of his argument for a moment. He attempts to remember.)*

JOSHUA. Maybe-

TEMPEST. Shh. Yeah, that's it... You look like a black man but you not, right?

JOSHUA. No, I am-

TEMPEST. I know what you say you are. Like you say I decide, not heaven.

JOSHUA. That's true.

TEMPEST. Then why ain't I up in heaven pitchin' pennies with Job right now?

JOSHUA. Because there's a difference in opinion over the state of your soul.

TEMPEST. And so where I go is up to somebody else?

JOSHUA. Your ascendance to the kingdom is up to us but the entrance to damnation, it seems, must be by your own choice.

TEMPEST. So that's the first lie. It's not up to me but to you. The second problem is this racism you puttin' on me.

JOSHUA. Racism? That is a complete fabrication. There is no race in heaven.

TEMPEST. We ain't in heaven, brother. This is New York City. This where I washed up through no fault of my own. Down here the color of your skin mean somethin'. An' the sin you say I did happened right here.

JOSHUA. So you're saying that you're innocent because you were born into a world that tested your virtue?

TEMPEST. Do only people who never sinned get to go to heaven?

JOSHUA. Of course not.

TEMPEST. So if a man or woman commits one sin but does five things good then maybe they get the green light from Saint Peter?

JOSHUA. Maybe.

TEMPEST. But if a man do twenty things good but commits twenty-one sins then he goes to hell?

JOSHUA. I don't know. There are no hard and fast rules.

TEMPEST. Them bullets struck me down was hard and fast enough. They hurt too.

JOSHUA. What is your point?

TEMPEST. You tell me I got free will, only if I try and use it you say the choice ain't up to me. You say I got the chance to prove my innocence but then turn around and say that they ain't no strict rules to say what's right and what's wrong. You show me the face of a black man then say that there ain't no race.

You talkin' 'bout the kingdom'a heaven when my kingdom is Lennox and one thirty-five. I don't want no Elysian Fields or Pearly Gates or angels' wings. I'll take me some chicken wings or a pretty girl's pearly smile. I'll take a football field. But I never asked for you to judge me...

(TEMPEST is suddenly struck by a thought.)

Hey... maybe you not down here judgin' me at all. Maybe it's me judgin' you.

(The ANGEL pushes his chair back a few inches. The lights hone down slowly until they shine only on these two.)

JOSHUA. That's ridiculous.

TEMPEST. Why? I'm the one said no and stopped the train'a heaven.

(TEMPEST stands. JOSHUA does too. TEMPEST approaches the angel who, through an act of will, holds his ground.)

If I say that I reject your power to judge then your whole world might fall apart. If I said out loud-

JOSHUA. *(Celestial Voice.)* It is not so!

(TEMPEST is momentarily stymied by the celestial tones of heaven... but only just.)

TEMPEST. That Barry White voice don't bother me, Angel...

TEMPEST. *(cont.)* Maybe I don't have the power but neither am I the sinner you say I am. You think you could prove me wrong but you the one that's wrong. You, not me.

(Both **TEMPEST** *and the* **ANGEL** *are shaken by this encounter.* **JOSHUA** *is seeing a different man than the one he expected and* **TEMPEST** *is somewhat daunted by thepower of heaven.)*

*(***TEMPEST** *exits the stage leaving* **ANGEL** *to wonder.)*

END OF SCENE

Scene Six

(**JOSHUA ANGEL** *walks to the front of the stage with the spotlight on him. He looks out into the void, his hands held outward in supplication.*)

JOSHUA. Peter, you never said a word about this. If I didn't know better I would say that you lied. A little man, you said, a stupid man who stumbled through a loophole. A lump of black coal that only needs to be dropped in the fire. I'd be home in a month. He makes no earthly difference.... You never said that he is the being that they whisper about in the alleys of Limbo; the Eschaton of the Afterlife - his skin holding in its darkness the Twilight of the Gods. He's like a depth charge in a calm sea, a land mine on the Golden Path. And you, you gave no inkling that if I lose this battle there will be no home to return to, no choir or even the memory of who I was.

(Considers his supplicative hands.)

And now, with this human blood coursing through me, in this body that is dying even as it lives, I am no longer the sliver of omnipotence I once was. I have been stripped of heaven as Tempest's actions threaten to strip heaven from Man. Was this body your subtle warning?

*(Now **JOSHUA***'s vision rises up to the heavens as he addresses The Infinite itself.)*

JOSHUA. Your joke? How can I - now little more than man myself - save Eternity?

(He waits for an answer but it does not come.)

Won't You tell me? Won't You hold out Your hand to Your servant? Are You even there? Have You already been sundered by this mortal's heresy?

(No answer.)

JOSHUA. *(cont.)* No. If that were true I wouldn't, I couldn't even remember divinity. If You were gone the echoes of eternity would have fallen silent. No. I hear You even though You do not speak, even though I am now more clay than spirit.

(**JOSHUA ANGEL***'s eyes lower to the earth. His revelations here and now.*)

I have been transformed by Your infinite wisdom, and this mortal's will, from Accounting Angel to the Martyr of Heaven. Either Tempest will break or heaven shall fall. The weight of eternity lies on these weak, fleshy shoulders. You challenge me but I will not shirk my duty. I will not allow this clown to shout down all that we've built. He shall beg me for damnation before I'm through with him. And I will be back in Your bosom, safe from the petty, childish wants of bodies like this one.

The angel slowly gathers himself and then walks out of the spotlight. After a moment the stage goes black.

Scene Seven

(Back at RENO'S BAR AND RESTAURANT the **ANGEL** *is once again waiting for* **TEMPEST**. *He's muttering to himself, preparing for the confrontation. He takes a sip of wine, and then another.)*

*(***TEMPEST** *enters. He's in a somber mood himself. He walks up to* **JOSHUA**'s *table and takes a seat. They regard each other. The* **ANGEL** *pours a glass of wine for* **TEMPEST**. *The errant soul picks up the glass.)*

TEMPEST. I thought you forgot me, man.

JOSHUA. No, Mr. Landry. You are my number one, my only concern.

TEMPEST. It's been three months. I was surprised you had my number. I didn't even have a phone last time I saw you.

JOSHUA. I needed... some time to... review your files. When you finally agree to the weight of your sins I don't want you claiming that I was in error.

*(***JOSHUA** *pours himself a drink.)*

*(***TEMPEST** *is a bit intimidated by the* **ANGEL**'s *bravado.)*

TEMPEST. They let you drink this up in heaven?

JOSHUA. It's one of the few vices we're allowed, that and pipesmoking.

*(***TEMPEST** *downs his glass and* **JOSHUA** *pours another.)*

JOSHUA. Is anything wrong, Tempest?

TEMPEST. Is anything right? That's what you should be askin'. I only been back a few months but it feels like ten years, a whole lifetime.... My wife got a new man in her bed and my kids don't even know me.

JOSHUA. It's been more than three years since you died.

TEMPEST. But I ain't dead. I'm flesh and bone, needs and desires just like any other man. I love my kids and now they callin' Rix Mulgrew daddy.

JOSHUA. Children need a father.

TEMPEST. I'm here, ain't I? I took an apartment in my old
buildin' and tried to talk to the kids a couple'a times
but they run away from me. That's when Rix Mulgrew
come down an' said to stay away from Jamal and K'nesa
or he was gonna call the police...on me! Their father.

(TEMPEST *finishes his wine and the* ANGEL *pours him
another.*)

Here I am, dead to the world but still breathin'.

JOSHUA. *(whispery Celestial Voice)* Then why do you insist on
staying? There's a place waiting for you.

(TEMPEST *looks up at the* ANGEL, *who holds out the
hand of heavenly damnation. Maybe* TEMPEST *is going
to take that hand.*)

TEMPEST. No. Why should I pay for them cops shootin' me
down? Why should I pay the price when Linda turn
her back on me, an' Alfreda treat me like she do?

JOSHUA. Alfreda? Your old girlfriend? What does she have
to do with this?

TEMPEST. She wasn't at her old place but I asked a neighbor where she gone to. They told me that she moved
out to Vinegar Hill in Brooklyn and that she worked
at a ice cream stand over near the river, under the
Brooklyn Bridge. I went there that very day, right after
my dishwashin' shift.

JOSHUA. Did she know you?

TEMPEST. No, but I had a story for her...

(TEMPEST *stands up from the table. As he does this the
lights come up on the other half of the stage. The front
of this space is the apartment with a table, chair, and a
sofa-bed; the back is an empty, undefined space. In this
space stands* ALFREDA ROBINS *in a waitress uniform.
She smiles as* TEMPEST *goes toward her.*)

I told her that I had seen her working in a beauty shop
on Lennox. I said that I had been sick and gone down
to South Carolina to get better. Now Alfreda is from
South Carolina and so we had a lot to talk about.

(to **ALFREDA***)*

I told her how I came back and searched her down because it was her face that came to me when I was really low.

(They kiss.)

(to **ANGEL***)*

One thing led to another...

(The couple walk into the apartment and settle, lovebirds on the sofa.)

...and the next thing you know we was gettin' comfortable.

(The lights dim on **ALFREDA***'s studio.)*

Now Alfreda is not a promiscuous woman but she knows what she likes.

JOSHUA. That doesn't sound lonely to me.

TEMPEST. You wouldn't think so, now would you?

(The lights come up on **ALFREDA***'s apartment. The bed has been folded out.* **TEMPEST** *and* **ALFREDA** *are under the covers, seemingly naked, entwined in each others' arms.)*

It was all going wonderfully well until she said...

ALFREDA. ...Roger Jones, you are the best lover I have evah known.

*(***TEMPEST** *breaks the embrace and moves to the center.)*

JOSHUA. What could be wrong with that?

*(***TEMPEST** *is standing half way between* **ALFREDA** *and* **JOSHUA***.)*

TEMPEST. What about me? Not me here but the old me – Tempest Landry before he died. I had been her lover for a long time, years, and here she meets some man on the street and in one night she's claimin' he's the best she evah had.

ALFREDA. Come back to bed, baby.

TEMPEST. I asked her…What about the men you known in the past? An' she said…

ALFREDA. …you are my soulmate.

JOSHUA. So you're jealous of yourself?

TEMPEST. My name never even come up in conversation.

JOSHUA. I guess that must feel terrible.

TEMPEST. You *guess*? Don't you know how it feels when a woman breaks your heart?

JOSHUA. There are no women in Heaven. No men for that matter. Angels are masculine but sexless.

TEMPEST. So you don't have no girlfriends? No marriage? No baby angels?

JOSHUA. No.

TEMPEST. Then how can you even think to pass judgement on adultery or covetin' some neighbor's wife's ass?

JOSHUA. One does not have to commit murder to judge a murderer.

TEMPEST. But you got to know passion and rage. You got to know when a man get pushed so far that he acts from his heart and not from sin.

JOSHUA. We have studied passion.

TEMPEST. Studied? You gonna have to feel it if you want me to say that I agree with your verdict on my butt.

JOSHUA. I don't understand. How can you question thousands of years an eternity of experience?

TEMPEST. Let me tell you somethin'. A long time ago I was walkin' down the street and I passed this poor white woman sittin' on the curb with three babies around her. She was askin' for some money to feed them cryin' kids. The crowd passed her by. I did too. But half a block away I hear these two fancy ladies sayin' how she should get a job and the state should take them kids. Now how's a woman wit' three babies gonna get a job? And what could the state do when them kids got a mother they love? I went back and give the woman half the money in my pockets.

JOSHUA. I noted that act of charity in your file but what does it have to do with my feelings?

TEMPEST. You like them fancy women - pass judgement on my heart when you don't know a damn thing.

JOSHUA. I am what I am.

TEMPEST. Maybe so but that's a human body you wearin' right now ain't it, Angel?

JOSHUA. Yes.

TEMPEST. Fully functioning?

JOSHUA. Yes.

TEMPEST. So at least you have the potential to know what it feel like to be a man.

JOSHUA. I suppose.

TEMPEST. All right. While you testin' me maybe I could test you.

JOSHUA. I represent the Infinite, the sum of all experience. What can you show someone who has seen everything?

TEMPEST. I don't need everything, Angel. Naw. All I need is a slugger's chance.

(**TEMPEST** *stands up, smiling.*)

Yeah…And I know just the thing too. It's time for me to go. Thank you, Angel.

JOSHUA. For what?

TEMPEST. I don't know exactly but it feels like sumpin', sumpin' good.

(**TEMPEST** *begins walking away from the table.*)

(*fade to black*)

Scene Eight

(Angel's small and cramped office at the firm of Rendell, Chin, and Akbar. **JOSHUA ANGEL** *is sitting, working almost desperately at an overflowing and disheveled desk.)*

(The phone rings.)

JOSHUA. Rendell, Chin, and Akbar accounting services... What?... No. This is an office number, not your girlfriend's apartment... What's your name?... Thom Lorring? T-H-O-M? I remember that name. You live at 79th and Amsterdam?... Yes. I believe your girlfriend is having an affair with a man named Justin Teegs. At least she was before I took this job... Up my what? Listen, Thom I have to go. I'm way behind on my work and this really is a wrong number... What? You're going to kill her? Then shouldn't she kill you for fathering her best friend's child?

(A voice comes over the intercom.)

MR. CHIN. *(offstage)* Angel!

JOSHUA. Yes, Mr. Chin.

MR. CHIN. *(offstage)* Where are the Lambert tax returns?

JOSHUA. I'm working on them, sir.

MR. CHIN *(offstage)* Working? You should have been finished with them last week.

JOSHUA. There were some fine points that didn't work out perfectly, sir. He, he claimed that his home office was a fifth of his rent but the schematics of the building...

*(**JOSHUA** pulls out a blueprint from piles of paper on his desk. Other files cascade to the floor.)*

...clearly show that his office space could be no more than sixteen percent. He also claimed a taxi receipt on December fourteenth that I...

MR. CHIN. *(offstage)* Have the finished return on my desk by nine tomorrow morning or you're fired.

JOSHUA. Yes, sir.

(JOSHUA is daunted by the work before him, overwhelmed.)

How do human beings get anything done with the clock ticking, ticking?

(The receptionist, DARLENE's voice comes over the intercom.)

DARLENE. *(offstage)* Mr. Angel, call on line one.

(JOSHUA picks up the phone and as he does a spotlight illuminates TEMPEST standing at a pay phone at the periphery of the stage.)

JOSHUA. Rendell, Chin, and Akbar accounting services. Joshua Angel speaking.

TEMPEST. You sound like a regular United Nations over there, Angel.

JOSHUA. Tempest.

TEMPEST. I don't have much time, brother. But I got somethin' I wanna talk about. Can you meet me at the inside public space at the Citicorp building after work?

JOSHUA. I'm behind here. As it is I'll have to work all night.

TEMPEST. I thought I was your job.

(The ANGEL looks forlorn at the piles on his desk.)

JOSHUA. I'll be there.

TEMPEST. You'll know me because I'll have a yellow feather in my hatband.

JOSHUA. Yellow feather? Hatband? I already know what you look like, Tempest.

(TEMPEST hangs up the phone and the light on him dies.)

MR. AKBAR. *(offstage)* Angel!

JOSHUA. Yes, Mr. Akbar.

MR. AKBAR. *(offstage)* I don't see the Lupinski files in my in-box. You were supposed to have them to me three weeks ago…

(As the next partner berates ANGEL the lights dim.)

(transition to:)

Scene Nine

(Lights come up on the interior space of the Citicorp building designed for the weary midtown traveler to rest.)

(There are a few empty tables and one with a mendicant sitting, guarding a shopping cart which holds the sum of his life.)

(JOSHUA ANGEL is sitting at another table reading a newspaper.)

(A lovely young black woman [BRANWYN WEEKS] enters. She's wearing an adequate medium brown dress-suit with a blue hat that has a large yellow feather stuck in the hatband. She looks around the room. Her gaze keeps coming back to JOSHUA.)

(He notices her but turns away whenever she looks in his direction.)

(She wanders around getting closer and closer to ANGEL. Finally she's near enough to speak.)

BRANWYN. Excuse me.

JOSHUA. Yes?

BRANWYN. Are you Mr. Sinseeker?

JOSHUA. No. My name is Angel, Joshua Angel. You must be looking for somebody else.

BRANWYN. Oh…My friend wanted me to talk to this man Sinseeker for him. He says he owes him some money over a bet or something, and he wanted me to ask him to wait till tomorrow.

JOSHUA. Why couldn't your friend come himself?

BRANWYN. My name is Branwyn Weeks.

JOSHUA. Pleased to meet you, Miss Weeks.

BRANWYN. You have a beautiful voice, Mr. Angel. Do you sing?

JOSHUA. I used to be in a choir.

BRANWYN. Washin' dishes.

JOSHUA. What?

BRANWYN. My friend, he's working overtime washin' dishes to pay off his debt.

JOSHUA. Well…good luck, Miss Weeks.

BRANWYN. You can call me Brownie. Everybody does. Even my mama and she the one named me Branwyn. That's a Welsh name. My mama said she thought it was so beautiful when she heard it that she had to have a daughter to give her that name.

JOSHUA. *(with feeling)* It's a beautiful name. Ancient.

BRANWYN. Thank you.

(**BRANWYN** *takes a seat at* **JOSHUA**'s *table.*)

Are you waiting for somebody, Mr. Angel?

JOSHUA. Yes, I am.

BRANWYN. A girlfriend?

JOSHUA. A man.

BRANWYN. Well…I guess we could wait together.

(*There's an uncomfortable moment for the* **ANGEL** *here. There's a definite, low key electricity between them and* **ANGEL** *is not used to such feelings. He clears his throat.*)

JOSHUA. What's your friend's name?

BRANWYN. His name is Roger Jones but he likes me to call him Tempest. That's his nickname. He's a really good man. I mean, I wouldn't go to meet some stranger that he owed money unless I owed him somethin'.

JOSHUA. What do you owe him?

BRANWYN. My boyfriend, ex-boyfriend, used to beat on me. The last time he messed me up so bad that I ran away but didn't have no place to go. Tempest found me on the street and saved my life.

JOSHUA. What about your family? Why didn't they help?

BRANWYN. I was too ashamed. I was all bruised in my face with two'a my teeth broke out. And I was real skinny 'cause I was hurt on the inside an' food just went right through me. But then Tempest found me an' got me into a hospital with a….

(BRANWYN stops talking.)

JOSHUA. With a what?

BRANWYN. Are you here for Tempest, Mr. Angel?

JOSHUA. Yes, I am.

BRANWYN. Why he call you Sinseeker?

JOSHUA. It's a joke between us.

BRANWYN. Oh. And do he owe you money?

JOSHUA. There's a debt that we have to negotiate.

BRANWYN. He got a insurance card from a pickpocket he knows and used it to fool the hospital into thinkin' that the woman on the card was me. He brought me in on a Friday night so that I could stay three days before the finance office found out. I had a ruptured spleen and after they operated Tempest took me home to my mama. The doctor said I would'a died without that operation.

JOSHUA. Did you pay the hospital back for the insurance Tempest stole?

BRANWYN. The operation cost thirty-seven thousand dollars and that don't even include the room. I only make six twenty-nine a hour at my supermarket job. And they don't give health benefits till you worked there six months. And even if I got the insurance they wouldn't pay for old debts anyway.

(JOSHUA and BRANWYN are facing each other and have moved closer together.)

Do you think I'm awful for wanting to live?

JOSHUA. No.

(He is surprised by this realization.)

BRANWYN. Can Tempest come talk to you tomorrow?

(She puts her hand on his. He is startled and moved by this physical contact.)

JOSHUA. *(whispering)* Yes.

BRANWYN. You tremblin', Mr. Angel.

JOSHUA. I should go.

BRANWYN. Really? Don't you wanna sit and talk for a while? I like talkin' to people. My mama says I talk too much. When I was a kid my daddy used to say he'd gimme twenty dollars if I could stay quiet for just ten minutes but I never could. I like talkin' to people.

JOSHUA. I don't know what to say. I've already told you that I'll wait for Tempest.

BRANWYN. I can feel it that you wanna stay, Mr. Angel. Maybe, maybe we could go see a movie or sumpin'.

JOSHUA. A movie?

(transition to:)

Scene Ten

(**ANGEL** *and* **BRANWYN** *are approaching her apartment door. They aren't touching but are physically very close.*)

JOSHUA. That was really wonderful. Wonderful. Filled with wonder.

BRANWYN. It was just a stupid movie, Joshua.

JOSHUA. Yes, it was but…the room was so big and dark and cool. The picture was huge and the sound made everything seem bigger than life itself.

(*They get to her door.*)

BRANWYN. You sound like you never been to a movie before.

(*They're very close now.* **BRANWYN** *is expecting a kiss.* **JOSHUA** *likes the closeness but doesn't know about kissing, not like this.*)

JOSHUA. I've never –

(**BRANWYN** *kisses him gently.* **JOSHUA** *touches his lips and then hers, almost like an infant discovering the pleasure of his mother's love.*)

(*The next kiss is passionate. After,* **JOSHUA** *pulls away. He's excited and aghast by this exquisite perfidy.* **BRANWYN** *does not see his crisis of faith and moves forward to put her arms around him. She kisses him once, twice, three times. Each osculation a nail in the body of ecstasy.*)

BRANWYN. My roommate's prob'ly in bed but if we quiet you could come in…for a while.

JOSHUA. I –

BRANWYN. I wouldn't ask just any man to come in the first day I met'im, but I can tell that you're a gentleman that wouldn't take advantage of a kiss.

(**BRANWYN** *and* **JOSHUA** *gaze into each other's eyes. In any other scene like this they would fall into each others' arms and stagger, a four legged beast, into bed…But*

JOSHUA *groans in misery and pulls away. He moves a step and half back from her.)*

BRANWYN. *(cont.)* What's wrong, Joshua?

(She takes a step toward him but he holds up a hand, arresting her.)

JOSHUA. I've never…I can't…I cannot…

*(**ANGEL** lurches away assailed by passions that he's never felt before.)*

BRANWYN. Joshua!

*(He exits the stage, leaving **BRANWYN** confused and inexplicably bereft.)*

(blackout)

Scene Eleven

(Angel's small and cramped office at the firm of Rendell, Chin, and Akbar. **JOSHUA** *is sitting at his desk with his head in his hands.)*

MR. CHIN *(offstage)* Angel, where is the Lambert tax return?...Angel!

JOSHUA. Yes sir.

MR. CHIN. *(offstage)* Where are those returns?

JOSHUA. I'm almost finished with them, sir. Just a few more hours.

MR. CHIN. *(offstage)* I need those returns by the end of the day or I'll find somebody else to finish them.

JOSHUA. *(to himself)* Like Peter discarding souls on the eternal flames of Hell.

MR. CHIN. *(offstage)* What? What did you say, Angel?

JOSHUA. This afternoon, Mr. Chin. I'll have those returns for you this afternoon.

(He looks around his disaster of a desk with disdain.)

I am an angel. Perfection that has existed forever outside of time. Until now everything I have done has been faultless, flawless, impeccable. What is this woman? This thing in me like a tickle in my human throat, a spur in my human heart?

DARLENE. *(offstage)* Call on line seven, Mr. Angel.

JOSHUA. How can the omnipotent also be powerless?

DARLENE. *(offstage)* Mr. Angel...Line seven.

JOSHUA. What?

DARLENE. *(offstage)* You have a call on line seven.

*(***JOSHUA** *comes back to himself. He looks at the phone, then lifts the receiver.)*

JOSHUA. Rendell, Chin, and Akbar accounting services. Joshua Angel speaking.

(A spotlight illuminates **BRANWYN** *standing at a pay phone at the periphery. She's wearing the uniform of a supermarket checkout girl.)*

BRANWYN. Hi, Joshua.

JOSHUA. Branwyn?

BRANWYN. I'm sorry if I did something wrong last night. I usually don't even kiss a man on a first date. But…I don't know. I like you.

JOSHUA. You didn't do anything wrong, Brownie.

BRANWYN. You remember my nickname.

JOSHUA. And your brown eyes and the scar on your left palm from when you touched the stove when you were five. You, you liked grape Kool-Aid when you were little but when you got older you preferred lime flavor. Your soft lips and the scent of rose oil that you had on a spot between your breasts.

BRANWYN. My Breasts? Dog, Joshua, you talk more'n I do.

JOSHUA. I like you, too. I just don't have much experience with, with the opposite sex.

BRANWYN. You could'a fooled me. That was the nicest time I had in a long time.

(**JOSHUA** *wants to speak but is agitated in ways that he's never felt.*)

Joshua?

JOSHUA. How did you get this number, Branwyn?

BRANWYN. You told me where you worked, silly…I like it when you say my real name.

(**JOSHUA** *and* **BRANWYN** *have a moment of silent pleasure on the phone.*)

Can we see each other again if I promise not to try and kiss you?

JOSHUA. I'm sorry.

BRANWYN. That's okay…I guess I better go.

JOSHUA. No. I'm sorry that I ran away last night. Your kiss… it made me feel things I never felt. I can't feel.

BRANWYN. I don't understand.

JOSHUA. I want to see you again.

BRANWYN. You do?

JOSHUA. Yes.

BRANWYN. Okay.

(Again a short spate of silence.)

I gotta get back to work. You remember where?

JOSHUA. The Gristides on Washington Street in the West Village.

BRANWYN. I get off at six. Meet me aftah work. We can go get some coffee.

(When she hangs up the lights die on her leaving **JOSHUA** *holding the phone in his hand.)*

MR. CHIN. *(offstage)* Angel!

JOSHUA. *(grinning)* Yes, Mr. Chin. I'll be finished in under an hour. I will be leaving on time tonight.

(transition to:)

Scene Twelve

(*JOSHUA is hurrying down the street, briefcase in hand. He's happy, excited. He stops and looks up at the Heavens.*)

JOSHUA. Branwyn. Branwyn. What a beautiful name.

(*JOSHUA turns to continue on his way and runs into TEMPEST.*)

TEMPEST. Hey, hey, Angel. Where you off to in such a hurry?

JOSHUA. Tempest.

TEMPEST. I thought you worked late ev'ry night, man?

JOSHUA. I…Um…What are you doing here?

TEMPEST. I figure if I'ma get you to commute my sentence we got to talk.

JOSHUA. I thought we were getting together yesterday evening.

TEMPEST. Sorry 'bout that, Angel. I got tied up. I hope it wasn't a problem.

JOSHUA. No. I, I read the newspaper.

TEMPEST. That's all?

JOSHUA. When I realized you weren't going to show up, I… went to see a movie.

TEMPEST. What about that yellow feather?

JOSHUA. I thought you were joking. I have to go, Tempest.

TEMPEST. Where at? I'll go with you.

JOSHUA. No. Please. I want to go alone.

(*TEMPEST suspects something but he doesn't know what it is.*)

TEMPEST. If I asked you to let me go right now, Angel, would you release me from damnation?

(*The ANGEL is arrested by this tactic. He stops and thinks about the request.*)

JOSHUA. I have to go, Tempest. I'll see you this Saturday.

(*The ANGEL backs away, turns, and exits the stage leaving TEMPEST to wonder.*)

(*blackout*)

Scene Thirteen

(…a restaurant. **JOSHUA** *and* **BRANWYN** *are sitting across the table from each other. He offers to fill her wine glass but she puts up a hand to say no. He pours himself a glassful.)*

JOSHUA. You don't drink much.

BRANWYN. Wine puts me in the mood, Joshua. And you just gonna leave me at the front door.

*(***JOSHUA*** looks down.)*

You never had a girlfriend? Not even when you was in school?

JOSHUA. These past few weeks have been wonderful. The movies, the zoo, the Staten Island Ferry. But…I can't explain.

BRANWYN. Are you married?

(He shakes his head.)

You like boys?

(He takes her hand.)

JOSHUA. I like you. I've never felt like this before and I am…deeply confused. I'll understand if you want me to stop seeing you.

BRANWYN. That's okay, Joshua. We can just be friends if that's what you want. I like you, too.

(transition to:)

Scene Fourteen

*(**ANGEL***'s small and cramped office at the firm of Rendell, Chin, and Akbar. ***JOSHUA*** is sitting at his desk thinking. He presses the intercom button.)*

JOSHUA. Darlene?

(At the periphery lights come up on a young black woman sitting at a desk with seven phones on it.)

*(**DARLENE** is a youngish black woman, dressed on the sexy side of office garb.)*

DARLENE. Yes?

JOSHUA. Could you come to my office for a minute?

DARLENE. I'm not your personal assistant, Mr. Angel. I don't work for you. I answer the phone. If you have something for me just bring it out here and put it in my in basket and if you have something to ask –

JOSHUA. *(Celestial Voice)* Please.

*(**DARLENE** is startled and transformed by the celestial request.)*

DARLENE. Okay.

*(She gets up from her desk, hesitates, almost sits down but then makes her way to **ANGEL**'s office.)*

*(**JOSHUA** clears his throat after the obvious exertion.)*

I thought I said I wasn't coming in here.

JOSHUA. Have a seat, Miss Wilkins.

(She does, a little disoriented.)

I have a question of a personal nature.

DARLENE. I have a boyfriend.

JOSHUA. Yes. I know and I wanted to ask you something about a friend of mine. A woman named Brownie.

DARLENE. Yeah?

JOSHUA. My friend has a man friend. Not a boyfriend but they go out a lot, to the movies and like that… Well, you see, Brownie likes this man. She wants more. You know?

*(**DARLENE** makes a sound that at once agrees with and derides the question.)*

JOSHUA. *(cont.)* But the man has very little, if any, experience with women. He doesn't even kiss her.

DARLENE. Not even a kiss? What's wrong with him?

JOSHUA. He has strong feelings for her but he's never done anything like that before.

DARLENE. A virgin? Damn. I wish I could find a man like that. I could train him right.

JOSHUA. What should my friend do?

DARLENE. The woman or the man?

JOSHUA. Either.

DARLENE. Well…all a woman could do is put it out there that she wants a man, a real man, a whole man. And when she do that he got to know that if it ain't him it'll be somebody else.

JOSHUA. But…I'm pretty sure that she loves him.

DARLENE. The more she loves him the more she needs. And at night, in the dark, in the bed alone, that need don't have no face. Life is too short. A young woman can't sit on that feelin' he bring out in her. She need somebody to hold her.

JOSHUA. What do you mean life is short? What does time have to do with anything?

DARLENE. Time is everything, Mr. Angel. Before you know it a young woman gets old and tired. And if she doesn't find love in her youth, her springtime, then she'll just be old and alone.

JOSHUA. So you're saying that the feeling of love in her heart isn't enough?

DARLENE. No. She can't live on a feelin'. He got to go there with her or she needs some other man. Haven't you evah had a woman, Mr. Angel?

*(**JOSHUA** sits back in this chair making the question rhetorical.)*

(After a moment **DARLENE** *sits up straight as if coming out of a trance.)*

DARLENE. *(cont.)* What am I doin' in here?

JOSHUA. I called you and you came.

DARLENE. Why? I don't work for you.

*(***DARLENE*** *stands. She's suspicious but has nothing to hang it on.)*

Do you hear something?

JOSHUA. What?

DARLENE. Like a hum…a low hum singin' like.

JOSHUA. No.

DARLENE. Do you want anything from me?

*(***JOSHUA*** *looks at her but says nothing. She puts up a dismissive hand and exits, somewhat flustered by the experience.)*

JOSHUA. She needs him to go there…with her.

*(***JOSHUA*** *sits back and the lights begin to dim. Time passes. Slowly everything is dark except for the lamp on* **JOSHUA**'s *desk.)*

(He gets up and walks to the door of his office.)

She needs him to go there.

(He walks out.)

(blackout)

Scene Fifteen

(Once again **JOSHUA** *is approaching* **BRANWYN***'s door. He walks toward it slowly, with mortal trepidation. He's about to knock but doesn't. He turns away but doesn't get far. He goes back to the door.)*

JOSHUA. Okay. This is it. Just a knock and she will be in my arms. I can be with her and still do my job.

(He knocks.)

Branwyn, I am here…

(The door opens and **TEMPEST LANDRY** *comes out wearing only a towel about his waist.)*

TEMPEST. Angel…what you doin' here, man? I know we agreed to talk but I never expected you to follah me down when I was wit' my woman.

JOSHUA. Your woman?

*(***JOSHUA*** falls back a step.)*

TEMPEST. Yeah. My woman.

JOSHUA. Your woman?

*(***JOSHUA*** takes another step back.)*

TEMPEST. What's wrong with you, Angel? Here you backin' up an' you the one knocked on my door.

JOSHUA. *(in anguish)* No.

*(***JOSHUA*** turns away just as* **BRANWYN** *comes to the door dressed in a satiny, sheer nightgown.* **JOSHUA** *staggers away quickly.* **BRANWYN** *comes out into the hall as if to follow him.)*

BRANWYN. Joshua! Joshua, come back.

*(***TEMPEST*** comes out to stand beside* **BRANWYN***.)*

TEMPEST. What was that all about?

*(***BRANWYN*** turns to look* **TEMPEST** *in the eye.)*

BRANWYN. Well…

(blackout)

Scene Sixteen

(Lights come up on the interior of Reno's Bar And Restaurant. **TEMPEST** *and his* **ANGEL** *are sitting across from each other at their regular table. There's a half-empty bottle of wine between them and an edge to their conversation.)*

(They are drunk.)

JOSHUA. It's been a while since we've discussed your sins.

TEMPEST. You mean the damnation of a man's soul for just tryin' to make it in a world turnt against him.

JOSHUA. Regardless, you were a free agent at liberty to take any action you wished.

TEMPEST. Ever since I was a child I been butted and battered, kicked and stabbed…in the back. All that and I never asked for a bit of it. But still you sayin' I'm in control.

JOSHUA. The challenges you faced in life were opportunities, opportunities to do right.

TEMPEST. Maybe up in Heaven that makes sense. But down here if I smash this glass in your face you'd be mad enough to kill me. Now tell me if I'm a lie.

JOSHUA. I would not kill you.

TEMPEST. But would you strike me?

JOSHUA. Unless I was protecting myself from immediate harm I'd be wrong.

TEMPEST. But you'd want to.

JOSHUA. Temptation is not the problem. It is the act that counts.

TEMPEST. What about them cops murdered me?

JOSHUA. We've talked about that already.

TEMPEST. Shot me seventeen times. The four of 'em. How many of them would go to Heaven if they died today?

(The **ANGEL** *hesitates.)*

How many?

JOSHUA. The last time I looked three out of the four would gain the Kingdom immediately.

TEMPEST. They wouldn't even have to wait in line like I did?

(**JOSHUA** *shakes his head, no.*)

Three murderers get a forever vacation and the man they slaughtered, a man who never killed nobody, gets thrown down in the pit 'cause they killed him before his time.

JOSHUA. Don't you understand, Tempest? There is a greater purpose here, something beyond your simple complaints. While you sit there jabbering the firmament quakes. Your refusal to accept judgement could disrupt eternity.

TEMPEST. Have you slept with her?

JOSHUA. What?

TEMPEST. You heard me.

JOSHUA. I don't know what that has to do with, with…

TEMPEST. You haven't. If you had you'd be talkin' differently and she would, too – in my bed.

JOSHUA. I don't care about your relationship with Branwyn. Her time, when she is not with me, is her own.

TEMPEST. That must be the difference between a angel and a man. 'Cause I get mad even knowin' you out to dinner with her, that when she sees you she won't see me later that night. Man if I thought you was gettin' some action, I might lay siege to Heaven itself.

JOSHUA. You'd attempt to destroy everything for the love of a woman?

TEMPEST. Wouldn't you?

(*transition to:*)

Scene Seventeen

(Minimal light comes up on **JOSHUA**'s *studio apartment. This light is from the piece of the moon we can see through his small window. The door opens and light from the hall floods into the extraordinarily neat room.* **JOSHUA** *walks in flicking on the overhead light with a gesture, leaving the door open behind him. He drops his briefcase on the floor, shrugs off his jacket, dropping that too. He kicks off his shoes and goes to the window.)*

TEMPEST. *(V.O.)* Wouldn't you?

*(***JOSHUA** *tears open his shirt popping the buttons and revealing his chest.)*

JOSHUA. Would I? No. But I love her…

*(***BRANWYN** *takes a step from the shadows of the hallway into the room.)*

…Tempest has beaten me. He has made me selfish and mortal.

*(***BRANWYN** *walks up behind and touches him. He jumps from the unexpected touch. She grabs hold of his hand and slowly pulls him to her.)*

(They kiss. They embrace. They fall to the bed taking off their clothes and exploring their bodies.)

(As they begin to make love the light goes up on the hallway beyond the door.)

*(***TEMPEST** *is standing there, serious and angry. He takes a step toward the door. He takes a step into the room.)*

BRANWYN. Oh, Joshua!

(This cry sends **TEMPEST** *back a step.)*

I love you, baby.

(This claim sends the errant soul into retreat.)

(transition to:)

Scene Eighteen

(The sun floods into **JOSHUA**'s *apartment through the small window. He sits up with a smile on his face. The door is still open. He goes to close it and then comes back to bed. When he leans down to kiss* **BRANWYN**'s *lips she awakens and pulls him into a heartfelt embrace.)*

(They kiss again but then **JOSHUA** *sits up and away from her.)*

BRANWYN. What's wrong, baby?

JOSHUA. Tempest.

*(***BRANWYN** *sits up wrapping her naked body in the blankets. She reaches out and touches his face with real concern and love.)*

BRANWYN. That's why I love you, Joshua. You care about other people.

JOSHUA. But don't you love him, too?

BRANWYN. Yes, I love him. He saved my life. He's sweet and funny and he knows what I'm talkin' about when I only say a few words. He's good with children, and he never hit me, not once.

JOSHUA. So then why are you here with me?

BRANWYN. Because every time me an' Tempest was dancin' I'd close my eyes and be in your arms. Every time he nods and understands me I think about that silly look you get when you just don't know. Late at night when he squeeze me and say, what's my name? I have to think for a second to make sure I don't say, Joshua. I been wit' Tempest ev'ry other night for the last two months. Every time it gets better and every day I want you more.

JOSHUA. We have to tell him.

BRANWYN. I already did. Before I came here last night I called him and told him that I loved you.

JOSHUA. What did he say?

BRANWYN. That doesn't matter. He was mad and hurt but I know he'll get over it. Come here, baby. Gimme some'a that sugah I been so hungry for.

(They fall into each others' arms making love again. The lights dim.)

(transition to:)

Scene Nineteen

(Morning light is filtering in. There's a loud 'thunk' in the darkness. This awakens **JOSHUA**. *He rises from the bed.* **BRANWYN** *is still asleep.)*

(He opens the door seeking the source of the sound. He sees the knife in the door. There's a note stuck under the blade. As he begins reading out loud a light comes up on **TEMPEST**. *He's wearing a worn suit and carrying a battered suitcase. He seems to be gazing down on Joshua.)*

JOSHUA. Dear Angel, I love Branwyn more than any woman I ever knew. She's the only real person in my life, maybe ever...

*(***JOSHUA** *looks up from the paper in his hand at the sleeping woman. She shifts in her sleep. He goes back to reading.)*

...and when she told me that she was in love with you, that she couldn't help herself...

TEMPEST. ...my heart felt like that egg when they crack it open and say that's your brain on drugs.

I think it was dying that opened up my heart to Brownie. Dying made me realize how precious life is. That's why I saved her life and befriended so many other people that you never even knew about.

In my mind, I thought that she was the one who was supposed to make the decision about my soul. If she loved me and stayed with me I'da stood up against Heaven and stayed in the world. So when she turned away I figured that I was lost, that I would admit my sins and face the music. I knew that if I did that my soul would go to Hell but you'd have to go back to Heaven and so you would lose Branwyn, too.

*(***JOSHUA** *looks up above his head feeling, for the first time, the threat of Heaven. Then he looks back at the note.)*

I got down on my knees and called on the Infinite but then I said, I'll be damned if I let this bastard beat me. I wondered if Branwyn wasn't your test but mine. Maybe you took her from me to make me give up.

That's when I decided to go on a road trip, to go out into the world and see what I could see. But don't you worry, Joshua – I'm coming back at ya. You might think you beat me. You might believe that I'm just bug under your foot. But I will be back, Angel...

(BRANWYN rises happily from her sleep. She looks around smiling.)

TEMPEST. ...I'll come back at you and when I do I will have my shit together. I will beat you at your own game and you will have to give in and leave this world and its treasure for me....

BRANWYN. Joshua?

(He doesn't respond.)

BRANWYN. Joshua.

(He folds the paper and puts it in his pocket.)

BRANWYN. What you readin'?

JOSHUA. Nothing. Just a note from a friend.

BRANWYN. Come back to bed, baby. Come here to me.

(He takes a few steps toward BRANWYN in the bed.)

(TEMPEST steps away in the opposite direction.)

(JOSHUA and TEMPEST stop at the same time, and turn back to face one another.)

(On the turn: thunderous SFX.)

(quick blackout)

End of Act One

ACT TWO

Scene One

(A baby is cooing in the darkness making the gabbling noises of an infant talking to the world around it. After a few moments there's a complaint to these baby sounds and then crying, calling out in that darkness.)

JOSHUA. I'll take care of her, honey.

(JOSHUA ANGEL turns on a lamp and climbs out of bed. He goes to a crib in the center of the room, turns on the overhead light, and gets a cloth diaper from a shelf.)

Good morning, my little Tethamalanianti. How are you today?

(The crying turns back to cooing and then tapers off as JOSHUA changes his daughter's diapers, humming to her.)

(BRANWYN rises from her bed and goes to the sofa watching her man and her baby. When he's finished changing the baby, JOSHUA lifts her, swaddled in a baby blanket and carries her to BRANWYN who takes the child to her breast.)

BRANWYN. Hi, Titi. Did your daddy change you? Did he use a old cloth diaper with a safety pin instead of the disposable? He like a old man, ain't he?

JOSHUA. Just trying to be green.

BRANWYN. You just like old time things like Titi's name…

JOSHUA. Tethamalanianti.

BRANWYN. You explain to our child why you named her that.

JOSHUA. I've already told you why.

BRANWYN. Tell her.

JOSHUA. She's a baby.

BRANWYN. We both like to hear you talk.

> *(Looking at the babe in arms* **JOSHUA** *begins to speak in a muted version of his Celestial Voice.)*

JOSHUA. Your namesake was a Mayan Princess who lived many centuries ago. Her father had grown old and fearful. He began to believe that a king could live forever if he didn't have a male heir to inherit the crown. And so the king had his sons arrested for treason and held a trial sentencing them to death. The king's daughter, Tethamalanianti, defied his decree and freed her brothers, she led the castle guard in a revolt and overthrew and killed her father…She saved her brothers but was tried for treason because, even though she had done what was right, it was against the law to turn on the absolute monarch. Her eldest brother, who loved her more than anything, was forced to execute her. And when he stood over her on the sacrificial altar, holding a knife of bright silver and dark jade, she said to him, "We follow our destiny, brother. No greater love can we know."

> *(***BRANWYN*** *gasps and brings her hand to her chest.)*

BRANWYN. Every time I hear that story it touches my heart. How did you evah find out such a thing?

JOSHUA. I used to study history…before I found love.

> *(They kiss. They kiss again. He moves away, takes out a suit that's hanging neatly in the closet.)*

BRANWYN. Stay with me and Titi today, Joshua. We can go to the zoo.

JOSHUA. They won't pay me for another day off, honey. And we have the rent and our bills. So many bills. I don't know how anyone who's sick or old makes it.

> *(He puts on his pants.)*

BRANWYN. Oh, I forgot to tell you. We got a card from Tempest yesterday.

JOSHUA. Really?

BRANWYN. Yeah. He's in New Orleans. He says it's really hot down there. Said he thought you might like it. I didn't know you like the heat that much?

JOSHUA. It's just a joke we have. Did he say when he was coming back?

BRANWYN. No. He said that it's a crooked road he's on… sumpin' like that…but he'll be back sooner or later. I'm so happy that he's not mad anymore. I know what good friends you are.

JOSHUA. I have to get ready.

(He goes into the bathroom. **BRANWYN** *rocks her child and hums a lullaby. The lights go down until there is only a very weak light on* **JOSHUA** *in the bathroom. When he looks up his face suddenly, brightly illuminated.)*

(blackout)

Scene Two

(**JOSHUA**'s office is now neat and well-ordered. He has mastered his work and systematized the files.)

MR. AKBAR. (offstage) Angel.

JOSHUA. Yes, Mr. Akbar?

MR. AKBAR. (offstage) That work you did on the Billings return was wonderful. He wants us to be his primary accounting service now. Great job.

JOSHUA. Thank you, sir. And may I say that this has been a wonderful working for you. I know I was a little slow at first but now that I have the hang of it I think this might be the best job I've ever had.

(**DARLENE** appears at **JOSHUA**'s office door. She's dressed more conservatively. Her attitude is less brash, more professional.)

MR. AKBAR. (offstage) Keep up the good work and you'll make partner before long.

(**JOSHUA** is proud of himself, satisfied with his office and his work.)

(**DARLENE** takes a tentative step into his office.)

DARLENE. Mr. Angel?

JOSHUA. Yes, Darlene. What is it?

(**DARLENE** approaches **JOSHUA**'s desk a bit tentatively.)

DARLENE. I wanna tell you something that I don't really know.

JOSHUA. What do you mean?

DARLENE. A long time ago, last year, I opened my eyes and found myself sittin' right here at your desk. There was this sound in my head. It was somethin' I couldn't grab onto. I think I was a little rude but that was 'cause I didn't remember…And then, a few weeks later, I was walkin' by this church and I heard this singin' and I knew that the sound in my head was that singin'. Or maybe not the exact same sound I heard but like an echo…you know?

JOSHUA. Yes I do.

DARLENE. I joined the church right then and there and I been singin' in the choir. And I wanted to know…do you sing, Mr. Angel?

JOSHUA. I like to think that we're all born singing.

*(**DARLENE** smiles broadly at this declaration.)*

DARLENE. Do you think that you and, and Branwyn of course, would like to join our choir?

*(The phone rings – loud and jangling. The bliss of the moment is marred. **JOSHUA** turns to stare at the phone.)*

Do you, Mr. Angel?

*(The phone blares again. The **ANGEL** is visibly shaken.)*

JOSHUA. Sure, sure I will.

DARLENE. That's so wonderful. You can…

(The phone rings again.)

JOSHUA. Darlene, you'll have to excuse me. This is a very important call.

DARLENE. Oh. Okay. I'll give you the information later on.

(She begins moving toward the door. The phone rings again.)

JOSHUA. Yes. Later.

*(**DARLENE**, disconcerted by the turn of events, exits stage.)*

*(**JOSHUA** picks up the phone. As he does a spotlight goes up on **TEMPEST** dressed in nice suit, eating an apple. **TEMPEST** is on his new cell phone.)*

Hello?

TEMPEST. Hey, Angel. How's it goin', brother man?

JOSHUA. Tempest.

TEMPEST. I'm down here at Bryant Park on the Sixth Avenue side.

JOSHUA. You're in New York?

TEMPEST. Yeah. Come on down an' let's pick up where we left off.

(**TEMPEST** *disconnects and* **JOSHUA,** *more slowly, hangs up his phone. As the lights go down on* **JOSHUA**'s *office an extraordinarily well-dressed and dashing young white man walks up to* **TEMPEST**. *This is* **BASIL BOB**.)

BOB. Is he coming?

TEMPEST. Oh yeah.

(*blackout*)

Scene Three

(On a bench in Bryant Park sit **TEMPEST** *and* **BASIL BOB**. **TEMPEST** *has a small bag of apples on his lap. They're conversing lightly, waiting.)*

*(***JOSHUA*** *enters. He's looking for* **TEMPEST** *and sees him, with* **BOB**.)*

JOSHUA. What's this?

*(***TEMPEST*** *sees* **JOSHUA** *and comes to his feet, smiling.)*

TEMPEST. Angel. Good to see you, man.

(As they shake hands **JOSHUA**'s *eyes are on* **BOB**, *who rises and smiles.)*

Meet my friend Bob.

*(***BOB*** *extends his hand in an elegant and understated gesture.)*

Sit. Sit.

(They all sit on the bench with **TEMPEST**, *the gregarious host, in the center.)*

I met Bob down New Orleans about a week ago, right after I sent you and Branwyn a post card…How's Brownie?

JOSHUA. She's fine.

TEMPEST. And what about your daughter…um?

(He searches for the name.)

JOSHUA. Tethamalanianti.

*(***BOB*** *smiles broadly at this.)*

TEMPEST. Damn. She gonna have to get a college degree just to say her name.

JOSHUA. You from Louisiana, Bob?

BOB. Not originally, no.

TEMPEST. This man get around. Me too. I been to North Carolina, Atlanta, Miami Beach. Must'a hugged a hundred girls and chased every kiss with a shot'a bourbon.

TEMPEST. *(cont.)* I almost married this slow-eyed girl down in Memphis named Marlene. But she was wild and I needed to keep movin'. Day before the weddin' she was in bed wit' my best man and I was on a bus to New Orleans.

JOSHUA. I'm sorry about that.

TEMPEST. No need to be sorry. New Orleans was a great destination. They know how to party down there. I mean that flood hurt 'em, hurt 'em bad. But them people know how to have a good time.

*(**TEMPEST** is wistful for a moment.)*

I was feelin' pretty good down there but then I started thinking about the old days...you know, before I died.

JOSHUA. Tempest.

TEMPEST. What? Oh? You mean Bob? He knows the story.... I was thinkin' about my mother and brothers and sisters. About my wife...and how maybe I should'a spent more time with my kids. I thought about Harlem, sweet Harlem, and I knew that I had to come home.

I headed down to the bus station to hop a Greyhound and stopped into a bar to get me one'a them fancy New Orleans drinks. That's where I met Bob...

JOSHUA. Excuse me, but if you were a transient getting around by bus how can you afford these clothes and that emerald ring on your finger?

TEMPEST. That's all due to Bob here. You know he's a slick talker and a man with deep insights, and even deeper pockets. He offered to buy me a drink and before you know it I'm tellin' him my whole life story.

JOSHUA. Everything?

TEMPEST. From the doctor's slap to Saint Peter's damnation.

JOSHUA. This is not acceptable.

BOB. If Tempest here could refuse holy Peter's condemnatory judgement then it is obvious that you do not make the rules.

JOSHUA. What's your last name, Bob?

BOB. Bob is my last name. I use it because my first name is weak. I'm named after a distant cousin…Basil.

JOSHUA. Basil Bob?

(**JOSHUA** *rises to his feet.*)

Beelzebub?

BOB. At your service, Accounting Angel.

JOSHUA. Tempest, do realize who you've shared confidences with? That you're now in league with the devil?

TEMPEST. Calm down, Angel. I ain't in league with nobody. Bob offered to represent my case to you because he says he knows all the rules that you ain't sayin'. You can hardly blame a brother for talkin' to the man.

JOSHUA. This is no man. This is the demon.

TEMPEST. Ain't it him you say I belong wit'?

(**JOSHUA** *is stricken by this turn of events. He takes a step back and then holds his ground.* **BOB** *also rises.* **TEMPEST** *looks from one to the other.*)

I just wanna fair shake, Angel. I been shot down, robbed of my name and family, damned by the powers that be, and now you sleepin' in what should my bed, with my woman. All that and I'm the one on trial. At least I should have a decent lawyer.

(**JOSHUA** *absorbs these words as* **BOB** *moves close to* **TEMPEST**, *who also rises.*)

JOSHUA. *(to* **BOB***)* I will meet your challenge, Satan. I will argue against your lies and meet you guile with righteousness.

BOB. How quaint.

TEMPEST. Don't be upset, Angel. You got what you want. All I'm after is what's mines.

(*The* **DEVIL** *puts his hand on* **TEMPEST**'s *shoulder.*)

Bob's is lettin' me use a big brownstone he got up in Harlem. Got cable TV, Internet, an' everything. I'll send you a e-mail with the address and we could meet tomorrow 'bout six or so. Then we could get this bad boy on.

(BOB whispers something to TEMPEST and he laughs. They turn and walk away, exiting the stage. JOSHUA stands in the slowly dimming light. He's breathing hard and concentrated on his task.)

(The lights continue to dim until…)

(blackout)

Scene Four

(JOSHUA ANGEL approaches the door of a Harlem brownstone. He's wearing a suit and carrying a briefcase. He looks up at the address and waits a moment.)

JOSHUA. Yea though I walk through the valley of the shadow of death I shall fear no evil.

(He takes a step up the stairway and stops to look out into the middle distance.)

Is this really what you want, Peter? Your fact checker, your bean counter going head to head with the crown prince of Hell? How can I serve you when I am so overmatched? With so much at stake why have you chosen me? Or is it true what Tempest said? Am I being tested? Is it the faith of Heaven in itself on trial? Don't get me wrong. I am not faltering. I will not stand down from the demon but what can I do and what can this weak mortal do against such a power brought to bear in the world? This is not so mortal man being tempted but the fate of Heaven held in the balance. Won't you send your archangels to confront their brother? Won't you do something? Say something?

(JOSHUA waits but he is not answered.)

That's it then. There's nothing else to say.

(He ascends the stairs and presses the doorbell. The sound produced is reminiscent of a foghorn.)

(BOB enters the den. He's wearing a silk T-shirt and silk trousers [both black] with red shoes. There's a big and bright ruby ring on the pinky of his left hand. He goes to the door and opens up.)

BOB. Joshua. Welcome.

(JOSHUA nods acknowledging the pleasantry.)

Come on in.

(They walk into the garish and opulent room. JOSHUA obviously has distaste for the decor. The devil gestures toward a leopard-skin sofa chair.)

BOB. *(cont.)* Sit.

*(***JOSHUA*** settles while* **SATAN** *takes a seat made from a squatting polar bear.)*

JOSHUA. Your place?

BOB. Tempest is staying here while we're working together. In the meantime I'm making my home at the new Thai Royale at Union Square. It's really gorgeous. Have you ever stayed there?

JOSHUA. It's a little beyond my means.

BOB. Oh yes. Tempest was telling me. With all the resources of Heaven behind him the Accounting Angel has to work for bookkeepers and live in a sixth floor walk-up.

JOSHUA. Nothing wrong with honest labor.

*(***TEMPEST*** enters the room, unnoticed by the deities. He's wearing a black and red satin robe with bright yellow slippers.)*

BOB. Work is for suckers. There's enough wealth on Earth for all humanity to live with the minimum of effort but instead they sweat and strain going evermore into debt while beings like you and I pass judgement on them.

JOSHUA. We merely carry out our eternal tasks. Without us others would arise.

*(***TEMPEST*** strides into the room taking a seat on a couch made from a dead rhinoceros that looks to be reclining on its side.)*

TEMPEST. Damn. You two boys cain't hardly wait to get started, huh? I thought this was my case.

JOSHUA. You're making a mistake throwing in your lot with Bob here. He doesn't care about you.

TEMPEST. Listen here, Angel. Ain't nobody evah cared about me – 'cept maybe my mother. So what if Bob got a bone to pick with Heaven? All you guys ever did for me was call me a sinner and offer me a one way ticket to Hell.

JOSHUA. Your sins called for that sentence.

*(***BOB*** laughs.)*

TEMPEST. Bob says that he never expected to see me down in his neighborhood.

JOSHUA. You have to consider the source.

TEMPEST. People been sayin' the same thing about me my whole life.

JOSHUA. I understand. Having lived as a black man these past months I have some knowledge of this thing you call racism. Taxi cabs have passed me by. White women, and black ones too, sometimes look over their shoulders at me in fear. One of the clients at Rendell, Chin, and Akbar refused to have me work on his portfolio… I've experienced these reversals and have survived.

TEMPEST. It's one thing to spend a night in jail and another to live a life sentence in maximum security.

BOB. That's where I come in. I'm here to inform this poor soul of his rights. He's the first mortal to at least partially figure out that he has a say in the disposition of his immortal soul. I'm here to make sure that he knows everything.

JOSHUA. Everything is a big word.

BOB. He's afraid of you, did you know that, Tempest?

TEMPEST. He don't look scared.

BOB. Ah, but he is. Haven't you wondered why such an important angel has been assigned to your case? Because if you renounce Peter's decree all of Heaven would be turned on its head. Instead of telling a so-called sinner to go to Hell they would have to ask if he, or she, was willing to go. Old cases would be reopened. The boundary between so-called good and evil would be rent asunder. Any soul could pass between Heaven and Hell without permission or warrant.

(**JOSHUA** *is stiffening under this assault.*)

Renounce Peter's authority to judge you and Mr. Angel's soul will be sucked back up into Heaven. This sham of an inquisition will be over and you will have the beautiful Branwyn for yourself.

TEMPEST. Really?

BOB. Truly.

(**TEMPEST** *absorbs this information watching* **JOSHUA.** *Maybe for the first time the Harlemite realizes how powerful he truly is. But along with this sense of power comes suspicion.*)

TEMPEST. Let me ask you somethin', Bob. Do you know a man name of Elrod Jenkins?

BOB. Not off hand.

TEMPEST. Elrod was somethin'. He robbed and stole and raped both women and children. Lies flowed from his lips like water from the Mississippi.

BOB. An individual.

TEMPEST. I used to see him around. He was skinny and small – unlikely to overpower any man of his own age. They finally got him for the murder of a woman named Bertha Nolde and her three daughters – seven, nine, and three years of age. They say he killed Bertha last.

(**BOB**'s *perpetual smile has dimmed for the first time.*)

You sure you don't know him?

BOB. He may well be in my realm. Peter sends six out of every nine souls to me nowadays.

TEMPEST. That true, Angel?

(**JOSHUA** *shrugs, accepting the implied accusation.*)

How about a man named Benny Rogers? Where'd he end up at?

BOB. Another archfiend?

TEMPEST. Bertha's oldest. Took his father's name. At seventeen he robbed a store and got himself sent to prison with Elrod. They say he stabbed that li'l man a hunnert and sixty-two times. You know ole Elrod was very dead.

(**JOSHUA** *grins at this.*)

BOB. Without personal knowledge of either case I can assure you that Peter sent both souls to me.

TEMPEST. *(to* **JOSHUA***)* Is that right?

JOSHUA. Probably.

TEMPEST. *(to* **BOB***)* And if I renounce Peter completely then Elrod will be loosed on the virgins of Heaven?

BOB. He will be free as you are now free.

TEMPEST. But I ain't no sinner.

BOB. *(Celestial Voice)* Renounce the authority of Heaven.

TEMPEST. But if I did that what would I say to Benny and Bertha when I see'd 'em?

BOB. What do you care about them?

TEMPEST. I got to think about this, Bob. I mean I want to get out from under this judgement but if I got to free Elrod and a million more like him…I don't know if that's right.

BOB. Right? Was your murder right? Is the history of the black man in America right? Are the slums and the prisons and the poverty rolls right?

TEMPEST. I know what you mean, I do…but I didn't do none'a that. This here choice is up to me and just 'cause another man done me wrong don't mean I should be like him.

(There's a chirping sound. **TEMPEST** *realizes that it's his cell phone. He takes it out and answers.)*

Yeah?…Hey, baby…Right here on one thirty-eight… No. I'm alone…Yeah come on ovah.

*(***TEMPEST** *disconnects his phone and smiles.)*

Listen here, Bob, Angel. I got me a girl comin' over in a few minutes. Why don't you two show yourselves out and I'll call ya when we can continue this here riddle.

*(***TEMPEST** *stands walks offstage.)*

BOB. What just happened?

JOSHUA. I don't know. Maybe it's the ascendance of man.

(blackout)

Scene Five

(JOSHUA and BRANWYN's small studio apartment.
BRANWYN and TEMPEST are having a friendly conver-
sation sitting next to each other on a small sofa.)

BRANWYN. ...an' you been all over the country? You know
the farthest I evah been from home is Yonkers one day
wit' my uncle Thad.

That and the one time I took the Path Train to New
Jersey but that don't really count 'cause I just got on the
wrong train. I was supposed to be goin' up to Thirty-
third Street but got turnt around because this man was
gettin' arrested by the transit cops and they was bein'
really rough just 'cause he asked 'em what was they
arrestin' him for. I was about to say sumpin' to 'em but
the I said to myself, I said, 'Girl, you bettah just let well
enough alone.' But you know I was so upset that I went
the wrong way and ended up in Newark. That might
be farther away than Yonkers but I didn't go there on
purpose and I come right back so it don't really count.

(TEMPEST basks in the glow of her chattering.)

TEMPEST. You ain't missin' that much, Brownie. You know I
got Harlem in my bones. Every day I wasn't here was a
day I wasn't at home in my own skin.

(There's a brief silence when another conversation passes,
unspoken, between the ex-lovers.)

BRANWYN. I'm sorry I hurt you, Tempest. You know I will
always have love for you deep in my heart.

TEMPEST. I know, baby. And it did hurt, too. For a while
there I was so mad I couldn't see straight. I might'a
made a mistake or two.

BRANWYN. What kinda mistakes?

TEMPEST. That don't matter now. What matters is when
I sit here and see you and your beautiful daughter I
know you made the right choice and I wouldn't have it
any other way. If I'm not mistaken you'll be expectin'
another long-named child in seven months or so.

BRANWYN. How did you know? I haven't even told Joshua yet. He's been so worried lately. I think it must be money problems. I'd go out and get a job if it didn't cost more for day-care than I'd get for a paycheck.

TEMPEST. Joshua's been upset, huh?

BRANWYN. He's turnin' in the bed all night long, like a earthworm on the sidewalk in the sun. Sometime he even forget to fold his underwears.

TEMPEST. He is neat.

(**JOSHUA** *approaches the door to the apartment. He seems haggard, a wee bit disheveled.*)

BRANWYN. Sure is. You know sometime I see him checkin' the level on his water glass.

(*They both laugh. Their hands touch. Just at that moment* **JOSHUA** *walks in. He sees the two friends so intimate and happy.*)

TEMPEST. Hey, Angel.

JOSHUA. Hello.

(**BRANWYN** *jumps to her feet and goes toward* **JOSHUA**.)

BRANWYN. Isn't it wonderful, Joshua? Tempest has come home from a long trip and want to be friends again.

(*She goes to kiss her man, but he moves just a bit faster and picks up the baby out of her crib.* **BRANWYN** *feels the rebuff.*)

(*Looking down on his baby* **JOSHUA**'*s stern visage softens.*)

(**TEMPEST** *rises also.*)

TEMPEST. That's a beautiful child you got there, Angel.

JOSHUA. Yes. Yes, she is.

TEMPEST. Ain't no one can take that from you, brother.

(**JOSHUA** *hears the truth in these words. He hands Tethamalanianti to her mother and then kisses* **BRANWYN**.)

JOSHUA. (*to* **BRANWYN** *and* **TEMPEST**) I'm sorry.

BRANWYN. You men have a lotta catchin' up to do and me and Titi gotta play date with little Mr. Bobby Sanders on the third floor.

JOSHUA. You don't have to go, baby.

BRANWYN. I'll be back.

(She kisses her man and casts a glance at **TEMPEST**.*)*

See you two later.

(She walks toward the door and out. She goes into the hallway and exits stage right.)

End of Scene

Scene Six

(The men look at each other for a moment and then go to opposite seats as if this was all a formal plan made eons before they ever met.)

(They stare at each other gathering their strategies and courage.)

TEMPEST. That Branwyn better than the both of us put together.

JOSHUA. Why are you here in my home, Tempest?

TEMPEST. I come to see the big dog.

JOSHUA. What are you talking about?

TEMPEST. The big dog look at me and say, here this little island of a man in league with the devil, like some little island of a country lookin' to get itself a big bomb.

JOSHUA. You're the one with the power, not I.

TEMPEST. That's what America say. America gets all upset when a tiny little country got one bomb even though they got ten thousand bombs. America say, look at that country over there. They a threat to peace. But what choice do a tiny little man got than to get ahold'a what he could an' hope the roof don't blow off?

JOSHUA. You aren't making any sense, Mr. Landry.

TEMPEST. That's what Uncle Sam say, too. He say any country that build for war ain't makin' no sense.

*(**TEMPEST** is moved to his feet by the pressure he's describing.)*

I been readin' the paper lately, Angel. Now that I don't have to go to a job I sit up in that big house an' read two, three papers every mornin'. And you better believe I see you and me on one page after the other. Me up against the wall an' you commandin' the firin' squad.

JOSHUA. I'm not your enemy.

TEMPEST. That's what I say when I read about peoples dyin' from our bombs and guns, police actions and whatnot. I'm not the one killin' them peoples.

TEMPEST. *(cont.)* But when they get mad at me what can I say? They ask, did your country drop them bombs? An' I say, yeah, I guess. An' they ask, did your country kill my eighty-six year old grandmother? And I say I guess so but... They ask did I crush their young men into pulp and then tell 'em who their leaders should be? And all I can say is, it ain't me.

JOSHUA. What does any of this have to do with our business?

TEMPEST. You say that I'm a sinner and should accept my punishment. But ain't that exactly what the man with the dead grandmother be tellin' me?

JOSHUA. But you didn't kill his grandmother.

TEMPEST. Maybe not... maybe so... But now I got me a enemy and so I look around for a friend, a ally. And who do I see but Bob?

JOSHUA. But Bob is the greatest evil.

TEMPEST. That's what you say.

JOSHUA. But you were already free. Traveling the country, kissing girls, drinking whiskey.

TEMPEST. When you wake up in the mornin' what's the first thing you think, Angel?

(JOSHUA does not answer this question.)

TEMPEST. *(cont.)* That's okay. You don't have to say. I already know. You pray to God that I don't make a decision today. You pray for that because you love that woman and that child. You don't wanna be plucked outta your nest like a chicken for the slaughter. And every mornin' I wake up I got Hell hangin' ovah me – seventeen bullets aimed at my heart.

(JOSHUA averts his gaze from TEMPEST's.)

(TEMPEST is moved to his feet by the pressure he's describing.)

Tell me sumpin', Angel.

JOSHUA. What?

TEMPEST. If America was a man would Peter send him down below?

JOSHUA. I, I don't know. We've never discussed that concept in eternity.

TEMPEST. I didn't have no choice but to take Bob's help when he offered it. Either that or spend eternity in Hell.

JOSHUA. But he is Hell.

TEMPEST. That's where it get tricky...for both of us. The way I see it you done kicked me over the side of a cliff but I was quick enough and grabbed onto your leg. That's like America and the little country buildin' a bomb in the woodshed.

JOSHUA. Yes, I can see that. And I'm truly sorry, Tempest but there's nothing I can do to save either you or myself.

TEMPEST. Yeah. I thought that's what you'd say. I guess for men like you and me the only livin' we get is fightin' to stay alive.

(Both man and Angel consider this statement a moment. Finally TEMPEST *turns and walks toward the door. He opens the door.)*

JOSHUA. Tempest.

TEMPEST. Yeah?

JOSHUA. You, you called me a man.

*(***TEMPEST*** goes out the door and closes it.)*

(blackout)

Scene Seven

*(Weak light comes up on the **DEVIL**'s Brownstone in the early hours of the morning, before sunrise. **TEMPEST**, wearing his satin red and black robe, is pacing in the lamp-lit den while a yellow door in the cellar, many levels below, pulses with an evil light.)*

*(**JOSHUA** enters the stage and rushes up the stairs to **TEMPEST**'s front door. He presses the foghorn-like bell. **TEMPEST** is startled by the sound. With trepidation he makes his way to the door. He presses his ear against the wood.)*

*(**JOSHUA** sounds the horn again.)*

TEMPEST. Who's out there at this time'a mornin'?

JOSHUA. Joshua.

*(**TEMPEST** hurries to open the door. He grabs **JOSHUA** by the arms as if the accounting Angel were a lifeline.)*

TEMPEST. Is it really you, man? You ain't Bob in disguise are you? How'd you know I needed to talk?

*(Before **JOSHUA** can answer **TEMPEST** drags him into the devil's lair. He pulls him to the rhino-sofa and they both sit. **TEMPEST** is still holding on to **JOSHUA**.)*

How did you know I needed to talk to you? Is that some kind of magic angel thing?

JOSHUA. I came to tell you something, Tempest. I had a dream.

TEMPEST. A dream?

JOSHUA. Yes. You were taller than the sun and held the entire earth up above your head like a glass ball. You were going to throw it down but then you held it out into an eddy of gravity and let it float away on its orbit around the sun. As the planet moved away you were engulfed by darkness.

You were gone and I never got the chance to thank you for all that you shown me, and the gifts you gave.

TEMPEST. You come here at three o'clock in the mornin' over a dream?

JOSHUA. Branwyn is my dream. Tethamalanianti is my dream. And though I am assigned to strike you down and send you to Hell I cannot deny that you are the source of all my happiness.

TEMPEST. You got to be kiddin' me. I mean I know you love Brownie and the child but I thought you must'a hated livin' down here. I mean when I first met you it seemed like you wanted to crawl outta your own skin. Now you sayin' that you just as happy in a crowded subway train as you was in Heaven?

JOSHUA. I am more joyful now than ever.

(**TEMPEST** *shakes his head in disbelief. Then he looks away fearfully.*)

TEMPEST. Listen, Angel, I gotta problem and maybe you could help me seein' I made you so happy and all.

JOSHUA. What is it?

TEMPEST. Come with me.

(**TEMPEST** *leads* **JOSHUA** *toward the far edge of the Devil's Den toward a newly illuminated area. This area is an elevator car.*)

(*Lights go down on the Devil's Den.*)

JOSHUA. What is this?

TEMPEST. It's an elevator. It go down more'n a mile under the house to a little room. We got to go there for me to ask you my question.

(*They enter the cubicle and* **TEMPEST** *pushes a button.*)

(*As they descend, the lights shift to mimic the passing of floors.*)

(*The first floor passes.*)

If you like me so much are you still gonna try and trip me up and send my soul to Hell?

(*floor passes*)

JOSHUA. That is my purpose.

(floor passes)

TEMPEST. You could try'n fudge the records and go back an' tell Peter it was some kinda mistake.

(floor passes)

JOSHUA. It is not in my nature to lie to the Infinite.

TEMPEST. Damn, Angel…

(floor passes)

…you make it hard on a brother.

(Floors begin to pass more quickly. One, two, three…ten, twenty, thirty…)

*(Finally the floor descends and **TEMPEST** and **JOSHUA** come out of the elevator into a hallway leading to the basement.)*

(They come upon the darkly pulsing door.)

JOSHUA. What is this?

TEMPEST. Bob said that this was the doorway to Hell.

*(**JOSHUA** falls back a step.)*

He brought me down here and said that he'd been tryin' to get other souls to say no to Heaven but he couldn't. Then he said that he went back to the old books, older than the Bible. He said that he thought I might be the man who's called the Eschaton of the Afterlife, whatever that means. He said that only this E-man had the power to open that door and either accept Peter's judgement or release Hell on the world. He said if I didn't release him and his people that he would make sure that I suffered for all time.

*(**JOSHUA** moves further away from the door.)*

Can he do what he say?

JOSHUA. Yes. I mean, he cannot compel you to go but once you've accepted your sins as Peter has detailed them you will pass automatically through that door.

TEMPEST. Unless I open it right now and release all the demons of the deep.

JOSHUA. Yes.

TEMPEST. An' knowin' that you still won't fake my records like I did wit' Branwyn's insurance card?

JOSHUA. I cannot. There are rules.

TEMPEST. Fuck the rules. If I followed the rules Branwyn be dead. Your baby would'a never been born. Who cares about rules when it comes to doin' what's right?

(**JOSHUA** *turns away from the door and his friend.*)

(**TEMPEST** *goes to the door and places his hand on the knob.*)

You know what will happen if I pull this here open.

(**JOSHUA** *nods.*)

(**TEMPEST** *turns the knob.*)

(**JOSHUA** *turns away, closing his eyes.*)

JOSHUA. Good-bye.

(**TEMPEST** *moves as if to fling the door open wide…but he does not. Instead he starts laughing.*)

(**JOSHUA** *turns to regard his friend and nemesis.*)

What can you possibly find funny at a time like this?

TEMPEST. Do you see me, Angel?

JOSHUA. Of course I see you.

TEMPEST. Really? What do you see?

JOSHUA. A man wracked by spiritual pain and mortal fear. A man who holds the Celestial Eschaton in his hand.

TEMPEST. You got it part right. I am a man. And do you know how you can tell I am?

JOSHUA. Tell me.

TEMPEST. Because I'm damned if I do and damned if I don't.

(*The pulsing light behind the door begins to dim.*)

(TEMPEST laughs some more and moves toward the short corridor that leads to the elevator.)

(JOSHUA is frozen in place, watching this amazing soul.)

TEMPEST. *(cont.)* Come on, Angel, let's get us some breakfast on Bob's credit card…get us some pork sausage an' eggs an' let the world go on livin' at least one more day.

(The pulsing light behind the door dies.)

(They exit.)

(blackout)

Scene Eight

(Angel's small and cramped office at the firm of Rendell, Chin, and Akbar. **JOSHUA** *is sitting at his desk with his head in his hands.)*

(Angel's desk is getting disheveled again. He is haggard and maybe a little stunned.)

MR. CHIN. *(offstage)* Angel.

JOSHUA. Yes, Mr. Chin.

MR. CHIN. *(offstage)* I just had a meeting with a new client. He says that he's heard of your work and wants you as his new accountant.

JOSHUA. My plate is pretty full, sir.

MR. CHIN. *(offstage)* Empty it. This man is rich. Very, very rich.

JOSHUA. What's his name?

(While they are talking **BOB** *appears at* **JOSHUA***'s office door, unseen by* **JOSHUA***.)*

MR. CHIN. *(offstage)* Mr. Basil Bob recently from New Orleans. I'm sending him right over.

JOSHUA. Hold it, Mr. Chin. I'm busy right now. I'm not pre-pared to speak to anyone yet. Tell him to wait until tomorrow…no, no – next week.

BOB. Hello, Joshua.

*(***JOSHUA** *leaps to his feet, the fear of that yellow door still pressing in his mind.)*

JOSHUA. I thought that we were meeting with Tempest at five tomorrow afternoon.

BOB. I have come to make a deal with you, Accounting Angel.

JOSHUA. Heaven makes no deals with the pit.

BOB. You'll make this one. I want Tempest Landry's soul.

JOSHUA. I don't understand.

*(***BOB** *takes a seat in Joshua's visitor's chair.)*

BOB. A wise man once said that when the devil comes calling there's no question about his intentions.

(JOSHUA sits to keep from falling.)

JOSHUA. His soul is not mine to give. Though Peter has sentenced him to Hell, he has exercised his free will and all the power of Heaven has not been able to dislodge him.

BOB. Is this the same Heaven that defeated my limitless armies?

JOSHUA. The same.

BOB. Tempest offered to represent me.

JOSHUA. Represent you? In what way?

BOB. He said that you told him that any soul, while still alive, could repent. He suggested that I repent and throw myself upon your master's mercy. He offered to be the go-between to make peace between our tribes.

(JOSHUA is shaken by this. He tries to pour himself a glass of water but fails.)

JOSHUA. You, you aren't considering that option are you, Bob?

(For a moment the DEVIL is inscrutable. Unconsciously, JOSHUA folds his hands in prayer.)

BOB. Please forgive me…

(JOSHUA gasps and pushes his chair back from the desk.)

(BOB spits on the floor.)

…if I spit on the nigger's soul…. We have the same goal here, Angel. You want Tempest in Hell and so do I.

JOSHUA. But if he is sentenced to Hell, his power will be nullified. I thought you sought the demolition of Heaven?

BOB. I've had second thoughts. I like things the way they are. Your master gives me more than enough souls to play with. The riches of evil are boundless. What more could I hope to gain? Add that to the disrespect shown me by Black Landry with his nappy hair and liver lips thinking he can offer the king of Hades absolution.

While he made the offer bile rose in my gorge. I smiled at him and nodded and said, 'What an interesting idea.' To think that a mere mortal man, the descendent of slaves would dare to speak to me as if he were divine... No, Angel, his power will not be nullified. He will amuse me throughout eternity. I shall make him into the mud in slaughter and rape pens throughout the warring world so that he can feel the suffering of his worthless brethren. I will nail him to a cross made of the living bones of his parents and siblings and children... Tempest Landry's power will fuel an epoch of pain on earth all of which will flow though his frail, arrogant psyche.

All I need from you is one weakness, one chink in the armor of his so-called free will. That is your job isn't it, Joshua? To sunder his spirit and render him unto me.

JOSHUA. Yes...it is.

BOB. Then, Accounting Angel, do your duty – help me to break this soul.

JOSHUA. This is more your area of expertise than mine, Bob. Have you made him an offer?

BOB. I've tried but I can't get a hook into him.

JOSHUA. He took your brownstone.

BOB. Only after I agreed to accept the token rent of a dollar a year.

JOSHUA. You've given him beautiful women, I hear.

BOB. But he loves your woman and has satisfied himself with her happiness with you.

JOSHUA. The stipend you're giving him –

BOB. You're playing with me, Josh. You know that I have used all these tools and more to seduce the nigger...

(*JOSHUA recoils at the word.*)

What? Does my nomenclature offend? I hate him.

BOB. *(cont.)* In his life he has lied and given false testimony. He's stolen from the church but still when I make him an offer he manges to deny me every time. That is why you are here and why I hate him so. Help me, Joshua. It is your duty.

*(Now **JOSHUA***'s the one who has become inscrutable. He sits across from the demon pondering the conundrum of his situation.)*

Ask your masters if you don't trust me. They know what's at stake here.

JOSHUA. They have gone silent. I beseech them but they are as the stars: far away and confounding.

BOB. Maybe it's because you've taken a woman, fathered a child. Maybe they feel you worship life more than that which comes after.

*(**JOSHUA** doesn't like **BOB** talking about his family.)*

JOSHUA. I have only one thought of something Tempest might want.

*(**BOB** leans forward.)*

BOB. Tell me.

*(**JOSHUA** leans across the desk.)*

JOSHUA. I will whisper it so that no one else can hear.

*(**JOSHUA** looks up at heaven as though in fear. As **BOB***'s ear comes close to **JOSHUA***'s lips the lights dim. Just when **JOSHUA** begins to speak...)*

(transition to:)

Scene Nine

(Silence in the darkness for a beat, two, three... A light illuminates **BOB** *in the middle of a gurgling scream.)*

Scene Ten

(As the lights come up we find **TEMPEST** *sitting on a park bench. He has on jeans and a T-shirt, sandals with no socks. A* **WOMAN** *walks by dressed for office work. As she passes* **TEMPEST** *speaks.)*

TEMPEST. Hey, mama. You know you look too good to be cooped up in some office all day long.

*(***WOMAN** *stops and regards her admirer.)*

WOMAN. Oh? And where should I be?

TEMPEST. On this here bench right up next to me.

(The **WOMAN** *sucks a tooth and walks on, not unhappy with her brash suitor. As she exits stage* **JOSHUA** *enters.)*

TEMPEST. Hey, Angel.

*(***JOSHUA** *comes up and sits next to* **TEMPEST***.)*

Yo, man, I never knew you had no sense'a humor like that. You pulled the joke'a the year right there.

JOSHUA. I was merely trying to help Bob out. He said that he wanted something to offer you, something that you really wanted.

*(***TEMPEST** *laughs as if the joke had been retold. It hurts but he laughs anyway.)*

TEMPEST. How the Hell you come up with that?

JOSHUA. He wanted to know what to offer for your soul. He called you the, the N-word.

TEMPEST. Niggah? Bob called me a niggah? And what did you say?

JOSHUA. I said that your deepest desire was to escape from the racism that formed your existence. Therefore, I proposed, your greatest desire was to be white.

*(***TEMPEST** *howls with glee. He's never heard anything funnier in two lives.)*

TEMPEST. If you think I'm laughin' now you should'a heard me when Bob said it. I really thought he was jokin' till I seen that gold light bright up his eyes. Damn. I bet ain't nobody made a fool outta him in a thousand years.

JOSHUA. What did he say?

TEMPEST. He didn't say nuthin'. Grabbed me by my damned throat an' nearly choked me to death. I was dyin' but you know it was still so funny that I couldn't stop laughin'. Do I wanna be white? Damn, Angel, you truly are a funny man.

*(**TEMPEST** laughs some more and **JOSHUA**, with a bit of reserve, joins in with him.)*

(The laughter recedes leaving an air of the seriousness of the ramifications of Satan's ire.)

Bob's mad at me, Josh. He wanna take my soul an' drag it through the sewer. You know I break out in a cold sweat when I think about the things he could do to me.

JOSHUA. I tried to warn you. What will you do now?

TEMPEST. I don't know, brother. Maybe…maybe when he calm down I could reason with him.

*(**TEMPEST** looks up at **JOSHUA**. They both know this is a vain hope.)*

JOSHUA. He's going to be on you, Tempest.

TEMPEST. Yeah, I know. But it was almost worth it. To be the first man in a thousand years made the devil's ears turn red…Even if I do go to Hell I'll be like a rap star down there.

JOSHUA. You have to be careful, my friend.

TEMPEST. Yeah.

(transition to…)

Scene Eleven

(In the gloom, before the lights come up, **TEMPEST** *and* **BOB** *are conversing in the Devil's Den.)*

BOB. You must sign this document if you expect to keep getting my support.

TEMPEST. What does it say?

BOB. That you renounce the power of heaven in favor of Hades. You must sign it now and it need be sealed in blood.

TEMPEST. I ain't ready to sign it, Bob.

(The lights start to come up.)

BOB. You remember that yellow door don't you, Tempest?

TEMPEST. Sure I do.

BOB. It is in your dreams is it not?

TEMPEST. Yeah. I see men and women tortured there. People that have fallen. Baby-killers and dictators, poisoners and other people gone bad. I know they deserve it but still I feel sorry for all that sufferin'.

BOB. Then sign this paper and set them free.

TEMPEST. I...

BOB. What you have seen is only the outer edge suffering. The souls you've witnessed are merely feeling the pain that they have inflicted on others. As you go deeper you find the mutilations that I have wrought upon those that have raised my ire. You don't want me for an enemy, Tempest.

TEMPEST. I try every night, Bob. I go down there and put my hand on that knob. It feel like hot flesh. I try and open it but I cain't, man. I might be dead to the world but my children are here. My wife and mother and friends are here. All the people I ever knew. I am what I am, man. They say I belong with you but they wrong.

*(***BOB*** considers his unwilling client. He doesn't seem angry or put out.)*

BOB. I understand.

TEMPEST. You do?

(**BOB** *comes close to* **TEMPEST***. He putshis hand to the side of the mortal's face.*)

BOB. Yes.

(**BOB** *turns his back on* **TEMPEST** *staring out into an infinite void.*)

Leave these premises, Tempest Landry. Take only the clothes on your back and the frightened heart pounding in your chest.

TEMPEST. I'm sorry, Bob. I truly am. But you know I never called on you.

BOB. Go. And the next time you meet me tremble. Now we are enemies and a war will be waged on you: body and soul.

(**TEMPEST** *reaches out to* **BOB** *but cannot make himself touch him. Tentatively he goes to the door and then through it, all the time looking out for danger. When he believes the coast is clear he races down the stairs and off the stage exiting.*)

Scene Twelve

(Dim lights come up on **ALFREDA***'s room. She's watching a broad comedy on the TV set which illuminates her face and fills the room with canned laughter.)*

*(***TEMPEST** *enters carrying a knapsack with his head bowed down. He comes to* **ALFREDA***'s apartment door. He's about to knock and hesitates.)*

(He knocks softly. **ALFREDA** *reacts as if she's heard something but she's not exactly sure. She turns down the volume on the television set.)*

*(***TEMPEST** *knocks again. This time* **ALFREDA** *gets to her feet, not exactly sure that she heard something. She goes to the door.)*

ALFREDA. Somebody out there?

*(***TEMPEST** *mumbles something.)*

What?

TEMPEST. It's me, Alfreda.

*(***ALFREDA** *throws the locks and opens the door getting a good look at the poor soul.)*

ALFREDA. Well if it isn't Roger Jones, the man who ran from my bed.

TEMPEST. I'm sorry. I shouldn't have come.

*(***TEMPEST** *turns and takes a step or two away. Sensing his pain* **ALFREDA** *goes out after him.)*

ALFREDA. What's wrong, baby? You in some kinda trouble?

TEMPEST. I just need a place to stay for the night. I can sleep on the floor.

ALFREDA. Come on in.

*(***ALFREDA** *seats herself on the sofa and makes a place for him but he sits in the straight back chair across from her.)*

(They sit in silence for a few beats.)

Baby, what's wrong?

TEMPEST. I just gotta get outta town, Al baby.

ALFREDA. Al baby. Another man used to call me that. He was the only one ever came close to you in my heart.

TEMPEST. You only knew me one night, girl.

ALFREDA. Yeah…but at least I had a chance with you. Tempest was married.

*(**TEMPEST** takes this in understanding something about himself. After a moment he holds out a hand to her she caresses that hand.)*

TEMPEST. Watch your show, baby. I'm just gonna curl up on the floor. I'll be gone before you wake up in the morning.

*(**ALFREDA** shuts off the TV set leaving them in lamplight.)*

ALFREDA. Come here. Come on. I don't bite. Not unless you want me to.

*(**TEMPEST** goes to the sofa. The first kiss is soft and sweet.)*

I don't want you runnin' off aftah.

*(They kiss again. The embrace becomes passionate. They're taking off each others' clothes. **TEMPEST** lifts her in his arms and carries her off to bed. There they wrap around each other under the blankets. Two snakes entwining they move sinuously under the covers until at one point **TEMPEST** rises up on his knees and **ALFREDA**, unseen, bends down, her back toward him and the audience.)*

That's what I'm talkin' 'bout, daddy. You my man. Oh God, oh god, oh shit…

BOB. …that's the way I like it!

*(**TEMPEST** falls back away from the bed and **BOB** rises from where we thought **ALFREDA** was.)*

BOB. What? Don't you love me, Tempest?

*(Screaming **TEMPEST** runs from the apartment.)*

(blackout)

Scene Thirteen

(A phone rings in darkness. It rings again and again. Slowly amid the chatter of the clattery bell the lights go up. We see **TEMPEST**, *now dressed in rags, asleep on an uncomfortable wooden bench in Grand Central Station. There's a bank of pay phones behind him. He's sleeping fitfully, disturbed both by his dreams and the ringing phone.)*

(Finally **TEMPEST** *awakens and sits up. He picks up a half empty bottle of wine from the floor and drinks from it. The ringing is driving him crazy.)*

(He gets up and goes to the phone that's ringing. He picks it up.)

TEMPEST. This is a pay phone and it's late.

(The buzz of an unconnected line plays in his ear.)

(Another phone rings. He answers it -- another buzz. Another phone rings. And another. And another. By now **TEMPEST** *is afraid. He doesn't know whether to answer or not. Finally he girds himself and picks up a phone.)*

Hey, Bob.

BOB. *(offstage)* The six fifteen to Cincinnati won't get you away from me. Sooner or later you will give up hope completely and then you will beg me to take your soul. Like Judas you will shed this mortal coil and be damned for all time.

*(***TEMPEST** *takes the phone away from his ear and stares at it. He hangs it back in the cradle.)*

Do you fear me now, Tempest Landry?

TEMPEST. *(speaking to the Heavens)* Fear? Let me tell you somethin', Brother. I'm a black man in America. I know fear better than Amos knew Andy. Black men 'fraid'a muggers and policemen, bankers and bosses, terrorists and anti-terrorists, meter-readers and little old ladies. We 'fraid'a fine lookin' women and children look just like us walkin' down the street. Black man get scared when he cain't think'a nuthin' to be scared about. So when you put the pressure on me like this I start to feel good. 'cause you know I'm right at home with this kind of abuse.

(**TEMPEST** *is less certain than he sounds. He looks from side to side waiting for a reply. When one doesn't come he grabs his knapsack, replaces one of the phones into its cradle, deposits a coin and dials.*)

(*transition to:*)

Scene Fourteen

(Light comes up on a pay phone at the periphery of the stage. **TEMPEST** *is standing there entering a number.)*

(A phone rings and another light comes up on **JOSHUA ANGEL** *sitting at his desk at Rendell, Chin, and Akbar. The desk is cluttered again and* **JOSHUA** *seems to be pre-occupied with the work before him.)*

JOSHUA. Rendell, Chin, and Akbar accounting services. Joshua Angel speaking.

TEMPEST. Angel.

JOSHUA. Tempest. Where are you?

TEMPEST. Bob is on my ass just like you said, Angel. He houndin' me. Houndin' me. I'm homeless and broke and everywhere I turn he there, too.

(While he's talking **JOSHUA** *keeps fiddling with his files, moving papers from one place to the other.)*

JOSHUA. I'm so sorry, Tempest. In my time here on earth I've come to understand that you truly are a good man, that our judgment against you does not match the content of your soul.

TEMPEST. Can you help me, Joshua? Can you put in a good word for me?

JOSHUA. No.

*(***TEMPEST*** is bereft.)*

But I've been thinking. There may be one chance for you.

TEMPEST. What?

JOSHUA. Peter knows what I know. He's seen your travails through me. Maybe if you pray to him he might rescind his judgment.

TEMPEST. What do I have to do?

JOSHUA. Get down on your knees.

*(***TEMPEST*** does this.)*

Clasp your hands and say, I throw myself upon the

mercy of Heaven and I accept whatever judgement you give. Say that and mean it and hope for forgiveness.

TEMPEST. I throw myself...upon...I throw my soul...the mercy...forgive...

*(**TEMPEST** weeps.)*

*(A pile of papers fall from **JOSHUA**'s desk. He bends down behind the desk to pick them up.)*

I can't do it, Angel. I can't say the words. They won't come outta my mouth.

*(**JOSHUA** rises. He is now **BOB**.)*

BOB. Don't worry, my friend. You will say them. You will.

*(Lights go down on **BOB**. **TEMPEST** rises from his knees leaving the phone dangling down. His shoulders are slumped and his demeanor is that of defeat. He walks out of the light leaving for a beat before...)*

(blackout)

Scene Fifteen

(When the lights come up on the park. **TEMPEST** *is seated on the bench again dressed as he was in the first scene of the play. He's eating an apple and lost in thought.)*

(From the opposite side of the stage enter **JOSHUA** *and* **BRANWYN**. *They are walking slowly pushing a pram. She's beginning to show.* **JOSHUA** *is distracted, even worried.)*

BRANWYN. …was talking to Roberta and you know what she said? She said that Luvia's husband saw Tyrone Jenkins down at Michael Jordan's Steak House with Donald Ripperton's wife – Chevette. But I told Roberta that that wasn't none of her business and she didn't need to call anybody to them anything. I mean she don't know what's goin' on behind closed doors and in private conversation. Just 'cause she wanna talk she could mess up the lives of men and women, children too. Don't you think that's right, Joshua? Joshua. Baby.

JOSHUA. What? Yes, yes. Of course, Honey.

BRANWYN. What's wrong?

JOSHUA. I was just thinking…about Tempest.

BRANWYN. Have you heard from him recently?

JOSHUA. No. I think he's in trouble.

*(***BRANWYN** *stops and* **JOSHUA** *does too.)*

BRANWYN. If he is then we have to help him.

JOSHUA. He's gotten mixed up with some bad people, Brownie. I really don't know what we can do.

BRANWYN. Just tell me where he is and who's after him. Tempest saved my life. I can't let him down, not again.

TEMPEST. Hey, you two.

JOSHUA & BRANWYN. Tempest!

(They rush over to the bench.)

JOSHUA. What are you doing here?

TEMPEST. I know your route. I just set myself down an' waited.

BRANWYN. We're so happy to see you.

TEMPEST. You showin' a little bit there, Brownie.

BRANWYN. It's a boy.

TEMPEST. You gonna name him Mixlpiteronomy?

BRANWYN. We're gonna name him Tempest.

(*There's a moment of appreciation here.*)

TEMPEST. Brownie, I gotta talk to Joshua alone for a minute.

BRANWYN. All right. But you have to come ovah for dinner later on.

TEMPEST. You got it.

(**BRANWYN** *walks on with the carriage as the men watch her exit.*)

Have a seat, man.

(**JOSHUA** *does this.*)

JOSHUA. I was worried that the devil had done you harm.

TEMPEST. He sure wanted to. I'll give ya that much. Shit. Old Bob was on me like white on rice; like America on the Middle East; like new lovers on their first time.

JOSHUA. What happened?

TEMPEST. Bob was after me and try as I might I couldn't shake him. Even in the toilet I could hear him gurglin' way down in the commode. I was losin' it, Angel. I had almost give up hope. I couldn't sleep and I couldn't eat. I was walkin' the streets ready to run at the first sign'a Bob…

(**TEMPEST** *gets up from the bench while talking to* **JOSHUA** *and wanders over to the darkly lit corner [where the lights rise slightly].*)

I was walkin' down a street up north of City College hungry enough to eat raw chicken and scared enough to catch a heart attack…

(**BOB** *enters just behind* **TEMPEST**.)

TEMPEST. *(cont.)* …when all of a sudden I turnt around and faced…

*(***TEMPEST*** *turns.)*

Bob!

BOB. It's time, Tempest.

TEMPEST. You can't make me go.

BOB. You can't resist. Your resolve is gone, your strength drained away.

*(As ***BOB*** *speaks* ***TEMPEST*** *lowers to one knee and bows his head.* ***BOB*** *takes out the contract and holds it high.)*

Give in to me now, Tempest Landry. You no longer belong among the hopeful.

*(***TEMPEST*** *looks up at* ***BOB****, who hands down the parchment and a quill pen.* ***TEMPEST*** *takes both of these. He holds them, a defeated man in the presence of omnipotence. He tries to sign the contract and then looks at the pen.)*

TEMPEST. You don't have any ink.

*(***JOSHUA*** *stands up looking upon the scene that* ***TEMPEST*** *is obviously relating.)*

BOB. Use your blood.

*(***TEMPEST*** *looks at the quill pen a moment before jabbing it into the artery at his wrist. He positions the parchment to sign but is distracted by the blood dripping down from his hand. He is enthralled with the crimson flow.)*

TEMPEST. Blood…It's like when they shot me.

*(***TEMPEST*** *drops the pen to the floor. He stands.)*

BOB. What are you doing?

*(***TEMPEST*** *reads the document for the first time.)*

TEMPEST. I was just thinkin', Bob.

BOB. Call me master.

TEMPEST. That's just what I mean. You talk all big an' stuff. You ask me why would a big time angel like Joshua be down here tryin' to change my mind. But you bigger than any angel. You the top man on the bottom floor. And so I have to ask myself...

(SATAN *leans away slightly.*)

...why's the big man from Hell up here tryin' to bully a black man from the hood?

BOB. I am Satan. I am your master.

TEMPEST. Oh yeah. I know. You the master. That makes me a slave right?

BOB. Sign the contract. Give me your soul.

(**TEMPEST** *tears the contract in two and drops it to the street.*)

TEMPEST. The answer has to be that if I can destroy Heaven by denyin' it then I could do the same thing to you.

BOB. No.

(**TEMPEST** *takes a step forward.* **BOB** *stands his ground.*)

TEMPEST. One word from me and everything you built would fall to dust.

BOB. You cannot defy me. In all of existence I have no peer and only one superior.

TEMPEST. Maybe that's how it once was, Bob. But not no more.

(**BOB** *pulls another contract from his jacket pocket. He forces this on* **TEMPEST**.)

BOB. (*Celestial Voice*) Sign!

(**TEMPEST** *is bowed by this assault. He takes the contract and clutches it to his chest. He kneels and picks up the pen. But then, in an act of visible will, he stands drops both pen and parchment to the ground.*)

TEMPEST. Just one word.

(TEMPEST approaches BOB and the Angel of Hell falls to his knees.)

BOB. No…

(BOB backs away half a step. TEMPEST moves toward him in an aggressive stance.)

TEMPEST. That's all it's gonna take. Just a word and you will disappear from this world and the next.

(TEMPEST reaches out to the DEVIL touching him lightly. BOB's response is to yell out in the anticipation of pain. He falls to the ground, bestial, begging…)

BOB. Please, please spare me, Tempest Landry.

(TEMPEST looms over BOB. He's about to utter a phrase that will send the Lord of Evil to oblivion. Then TEMPEST has yet another realization. He does not speak the words that BOB dreads.)

TEMPEST. No. No, no, no.

(BOB cowers and falls back.)

(TEMPEST looks at his own hands as if there were great power in them.)

No. This is what Peter did to me, what you tried to do.

(TEMPEST holds up a bloody hand dripping his life's fluid onto the street.)

This is what makes life. This is what makes me and mine different than you, Bob. A man got somethin' at stake, somethin' that reminds him what life is all about. I'm a man and I always will be. I'm not the thing you try an' make outta me.

(BOB bows his head. In an act of unexpected kindness TEMPEST helps BOB to his feet.)

Go on now, get outta here. Leave me be.

(TEMPEST turns his back on BOB and walks back to the bench as the light goes down on BOB and the street.)

(JOSHUA heads back to the bench with TEMPEST.)

JOSHUA. So Bob is gone?

TEMPEST. Back in the pit with the different heads of the political parties past and present.

JOSHUA. Congratulations.

TEMPEST. For figurin' it out?

JOSHUA. You made a deal with the devil without selling your soul. That's another first.

TEMPEST. So…will Heaven make me the same deal?

(JOSHUA *shakes his head, no.*)

JOSHUA. Heaven cannot make deals. We either stand or fall by our beliefs. As far as we're concerned you are still Bob's subject, no matter what he says.

TEMPEST. But I don't have to go unless you prove me wrong.

JOSHUA. I will succeed at that task one day.

(TEMPEST *hands* JOSHUA *an apple from his sack.* JOSHUA *hesitates and then takes the fruit.*)

TEMPEST. When I saw you walkin' I could tell that you was still crazy 'bout Brownie and that little mouth full'a syllables.

JOSHUA. Moreso every day.

TEMPEST. I went back to see Alfreda…at least I think I did. You know, Angel, it ain't too bad bein' us.

JOSHUA. As long as it lasts.

TEMPEST. Hey, baby, now you beginnin' to understand what it's like bein' me.

End of Play

COSTUME PLOT

Act 1, sc. 1 -2 & Act 2, sc. 15	Khaki Slacks	
	Tan Jacket	REMOVED ON STAGE
	Shoes #1	
	Corn Row Wig	REMOVED ON STAGE
	Socks	
	Undershirt	
	Henley	
	Underwear	
Act 1, sc. 3 - 6	Khaki Slacks	REPEAT
	Tan Jacket w/ Bullet holes Shoes #1	REPEAT
	Socks	REPEAT
	Undershirt	REPEAT
	Henley	REPEAT
	Underwear	REPEAT
Act 1, sc. 7, 8, 12, 15, 16	Brown Cargo Pants	
	Print T-shirt	
	Print zip front Hoodie	
	Shoes #2	
	Socks	REPEAT
	Underwear	REPEAT
Act 1, sc. 18 - 19	REPEAT ALL ITEMS FROM COSTUME 3	
	ADD: Green Hooded Coat	
Act 2, sc. 2 - 3, 5 -6, 10 - 11	Pumpkin Suede cloth shirt	
	Pumpkin Suede cloth pants	
	Navy/Pumpkin jacket	
	Shoes #3	
	Socks	REPEAT
	Underwear	REPEAT
	Pumpkin Hat	

Act 2, sc. 4, 7	Pumpkin Suede cloth shirt	REPEAT
	Pumpkin Suede cloth pants	REPEAT
	Shoes #3	REPEAT
	Socks	REPEAT
	Underwear	REPEAT
	Maroon Dressing Gown	
Act 2, sc. 12 - 14	Pumpkin Suede cloth shirt (distressed)	
	Lt. grey sweatpants (distressed)	
	Grey/Brown Overcoat (distressed)	
	Socks	REPEAT
	Underwear	REPEAT
	Shoes #4	
Act 1, sc. 2	Blue Hooded caftan	
	Blue suit trousers	UNDERDRESSED
	Blue vest	UNDERDRESSED
	Blue shirt	UNDERDRESSED
	Blue tie	UNDERDRESSED
	Socks	
	Underwear	
	Undershirt	
	Blue Tooth Device on Ear	PROVIDED BY SOUND
	Brown Oxfords	
Act 1, sc. 3 - 19	Blue suit trousers	REPEAT
	Blue vest	REPEAT
	Blue DB suit jacket	
	Blue shirt	REPEAT
	Blue tie	REPEAT
	Socks	REPEAT
	Underwear	REPEAT
	Undershirt	REPEAT
	Blue Tooth Device	REPEAT
	Brown Oxfords	REPEAT

Act 2	Grey Striped suit trousers	
	Grey Striped vest	
	Grey Striped DB suit jacket	Preset On Stage for Act 2
	Grey Striped shirt	
	Socks	REPEAT
	Underwear	REPEAT
	Undershirt	REPEAT
	Blue Tooth Device	REPEAT
	Black Oxfords	
SAINT PETER	Tan/Gold Jumpsuit	
Act 1, sc. 2	Ivory/Gold pleated Tabard	
	Gold Miter	
	Socks	
	Underwear	
	Undershirt	
	Silver Shoes	
	Blue Tooth device	Provided by Sound
BOB as WAITER	Lavender shirt	
Act 1, sc. 4	Black pants	
	Waiter's apron	
	Long Wig	
	Silver/Rhinestone Ring	
	Socks	REPEAT
	Underwear	REPEAT
	Undershirt	REPEAT
	Snakeskin boots	
	Blue Tooth device	REPEAT
BOB as CITICORP MAN	Black/Grey striped shirt	
Act 1, sc. 9	Silver/Rhinestone Ring	REPEAT
	Black jeans (distressed)	
	Socks	REPEAT
	Underwear	REPEAT
	Undershirt	REPEAT
	Homeless Man shoe	
	Purple print scarf	Worn as scarf
	Black overcoat (distressed)	
	Long Wig	REPEAT
	Blue Tooth device	REPEAT

Character / Scene	Item	Note
BASIL BOB Act 1 , sc. 19 & Act 2, sc. 4, 7, 8, 11, 12	Plum/gold Shirt	REPEAT
	Silver/Rhinestone Ring	REPEAT
	Suede snakeskin print pants	
	Socks	REPEAT
	Underwear	REPEAT
	Undershirt	REPEAT
	Snakeskin boots	REPEAT
	Plum Suede Cutaway Coat	
	Long Wig	REPEAT
	Blue Tooth device	REPEAT
BASIL BOB Act 2, sc. 2 -3 , 15	Plum/gold Shirt	REPEAT
	Silver/Rhinestone Ring	REPEAT
	Socks	REPEAT
	Underwear	REPEAT
	Undershirt	REPEAT
	Snakeskin boots	REPEAT
	Long Wig	REPEAT
	Purple Velvet trousers	
	Purple Velvet jacket	
	Purple scarf	Worn as Necktie
	Brooch	Below knot of scarf
	Blue Tooth device	REPEAT
PENITENT 4 Act 1, sc. 2	Black mesh body brief	
	Black padded bra	
	Underwear	
	Black/Silver Platform Shoes	
	Ivory Hooded caftan	
	Black chiffon hood	
BRANWYN Act 1, sc. 9 -10	Black mesh body brief	REPEAT
	Black padded bra	REPEAT
	Underwear	REPEAT
	Red knit dress	
	Red hat w/ yellow feather	
	Long Hair Piece	
	Black/Silver Platform Shoes	REPEAT

Act 1, sc. 11	Black mesh body brief	
	Black padded bra	REPEAT
	Underwear	REPEAT
	Red knit dress	REPEAT
	Long Hair Piece	REPEAT
	Burgundy Short Sl. Blouse	
	Black/Silver Platform Shoes	REPEAT
Act 1, sc. 13	Black mesh body brief	REPEAT
	Black padded bra	
	Underwear	REPEAT
	Long Hair Piece	REPEAT
	Ivory Swirly Print Knit Dress	
	Black/Silver Platform Shoes	REPEAT
Act 1, sc. 15	Black mesh body brief	REPEAT
	Black padded bra	REPEAT
	Underwear	REPEAT
	Long Hair Piece	REPEAT
	Red/Black Print Negligee	Removed On Stage
	Red/Black Print Teddy	
	Shoes #2	
DARLENE	Black mesh body brief	
Act 1, sc. 3	Black padded bra	
	Underwear	
	Leopard print cowl sweater	
Act 1, sc. 17 -19	Black mesh body brief	REPEAT
	Black padded bra	REPEAT
	Underwear	REPEAT
	Long Hair Piece	REPEAT
	Red Teddy	
	Red Trench Coat	Removed On Stage
	Shoes #3	
Act 2, sc. 1 -5	Black mesh body brief	REPEAT
	Black padded bra	REPEAT
	Underwear	REPEAT
	Long Hair Piece	REPEAT
	Pants	
	Top	
	Shoes #4	REPEAT

Act 2, sc. 15	Black mesh body brief	REPEAT
	Black padded bra	REPEAT
	Underwear	REPEAT
	Long Hair Piece	
	Pregnancy Pad	
	Black leggings	
	Red/Black Maternity Top	
	Shoes #5	
	Bronze Jacket	
	Blue Jeans	
	Belt #1	
	Black/Gold boots	
	Wig #1 (Lt. Brown Asymmetrical Cut)	
	Gold Hoop Earrings	
	Leopard print Purse	
ALFREDA	Black mesh body brief	REPEAT
Act 1, sc. 7	Black padded bra	REPEAT
	Underwear	REPEAT
	Black mesh Teddy w/ Red/Black Cups	
	Red/Black Briefs	
	Wig #2 (Black/Burgundy shoulder length)	
DARLENE	Black mesh body brief	REPEAT
Act 1, sc. 14	Black padded bra	REPEAT
	Underwear	REPEAT
	Hot Pink Jeans	
	Purple print Pleated Top	
	Black/Gold boots	REPEAT
	Wig #1 (Lt. Brown Asymmetrical Cut)	
	Gold Hoop Earrings	REPEAT
DARLENE	Black mesh body brief	REPEAT
Act 2, sc. 2	Black padded bra	REPEAT
	Underwear	REPEAT
	Bright Pink Jump suit	
	Belt #2	
	Burgundy Suede Boots	
	Wig #1 (Lt. Brown Asymmetrical Cut)	REPEAT

DARLENE	Black mesh body brief	REPEAT
Act. 2, sc. 10	Black padded bra	REPEAT
	Underwear	REPEAT
	Orange/Brown Print Leotard	
	Orange Skirt	
	Lt. Brown Belt	
	Brown Skin Print Boots	
	Wig #1 (Lt. Brown Asymmetrical Cut)	REPEAT
AFREDA	Black mesh body brief	
Act. 2, sc. 12	Black padded bra	
	Underwear	
	Wig #2 (Black/Burgundy shoulder length)	
	Black Leggings	
	Purple/Green Print Top	
PENITENT	Undershirt	
Act 1, sc. 2	Socks	
	Black Leather Slip on Shoe	
	Blue Dress Shirt	Underdressed
	Black Trousers	Underdressed
	Black Belt	Underdressed
	Ivory Hooded Caftan	
	Black Chiffon Hood	
WAITER	Undershirt	REPEAT
Act 1, sc. 4, 7	Socks	REPEAT
	Black Leather Slip on Shoe	REPEAT
	Blue Dress Shirt	REPEAT
	Black Trousers	REPEAT
	Black Belt	REPEAT
	Waiter's Apron	
MAN 1	Undershirt	REPEAT
Act 1, sc. 9 - 11	Socks	REPEAT
	Black Leather Slip on Shoe	REPEAT
	Blue Dress Shirt	REPEAT
	Grey Zip Front Cardigan	
	Black Trousers	REPEAT
	Black Belt	REPEAT
	Grey Print Cap	

MAN 1	Undershirt	REPEAT
Act 2, sc. 2 - 3, 15	Socks	REPEAT
	Black Leather Slip on Shoe	REPEAT
	Blue/Grey Shirt	
	Black Trousers	REPEAT
	Grey Print Cap	REPEAT
	Leather Jacket	

PENITENT 2	Black mesh body briefer	
Act 1, sc. 2	black padded bra	
	Black skirt	Underdressed
	Turquoise Plaid Blouse	Underdressed
	Boots	
	Ivory Hooded Caftan	
	Black Chiffon Hood	

WOMAN	Black mesh body briefer	REPEAT
Act 1, sc. 1, 5, 9	black padded bra	REPEAT
	Black skirt	REPEAT
	Turquoise Plaid Blouse	REPEAT
	Boots	REPEAT
	Jeans Jacket	

WOMAN	Black mesh body briefer	REPEAT
Act 1, 2 - 3, 15	black padded bra	REPEAT
	Jeans w/ Cuts on Front Leg	
	Sequined Top	
	Jeans Jacket	REPEAT
	Boots	REPEAT

MAN 2	Undershirt	
Act 1, sc. 1, 9	Socks	
	Henley	
	Khaki pants	
	Belt	
	Zip Front Print Hoodie	
	Tan Jacket	
	Shoes #1	

PENITENT	Undershirt	REPEAT
Act 1, sc. 2	Socks	REPEAT
	Henley	REPEAT
	Khaki pants	REPEAT
	Belt	REPEAT
	Ivory Hooded caftan	
	Black chiffon hood	
	Shoes #1	REPEAT
MAN	Undershirt	
Act 2, sc. 2 - 3, 15	Socks	REPEAT
	Print T-shirt or Polo Shirt	REPEAT
	Shoes #1	REPEAT
	Jacket ??	
	Belt	REPEAT

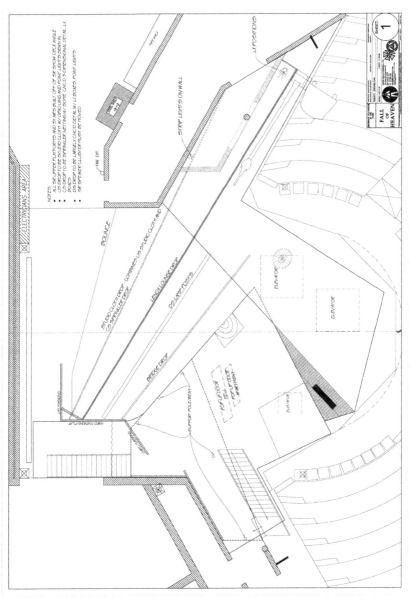

Set design by Thomas George

ABOUT THE PLAYWRIGHT

Walter Mosley is one of the most versatile and admired writers in America today. He is the author of more than 34 critically acclaimed books, including the major bestselling mystery series featuring Easy Rawlins. His work has been translated into 21 languages and includes literary fiction, science fiction, political monographs, and a young adult novel. His short fiction has been widely published, and his non-fiction has appeared in *The New York Times Magazine* and *The Nation*, among other publications.

Two movies have been made from his work including the 1995 TriStar release of *Devil in A Blue Dress*, produced by Jonathan Demme, directed by Carl Franklin, and starring Denzel Washington and Jennifer Beals. *Always Outnumbered*, was produced by HBO/NYC and Palomar Pictures film, directed by Michael Apted and starred Laurence Fishburne, Natalie Cole, Cicely Tyson and Bill Cobbs.

His first full-length play, *The Fall of Heaven*, adapted from his novel *The Tempest Tales*, received its World Premiere production at Cincinnati Playhouse in the Park, under Marion McClinton's direction. Of the production, critics hailed that "*The Fall of Heaven* could mark the rise of Walter Mosley as a powerful contemporary voice on the American stage."

Other plays currently in development include *Leading From the Affair, Lift,* and the musical adaptation of *Devil in a Blue Dress.*

Mosley has currently teamed up with Jonathan Demme to co-write a pilot for HBO based on Mosley's detective novel series *The Long Fall.* Mosley will be executive producer along with Demme, Tom Hanks, and Gary Goetzman.

Mosley is the winner of numerous awards, including an O. Henry Award, a Grammy, and PEN America's Lifetime Achievement Award.

A native of Los Angeles, he lives in New York City.

OTHER TITLES AVAILABLE FROM SAMUEL FRENCH

THE GOOD COUNSELOR

Kathryn Grant

Drama / 2m, 3f

The Good Counselor is a new drama about a chosen son's quest for truth. Vincent, a bright young lawyer in the Public Defender department has been assigned to defend a young woman accused of killing her three week-old son. Hounded by his community and haunted by his past, Vincent struggles to defend both neglectful mothers: his client, and his own. A thought-provoking and beautifully written play, *The Good Counselor* literally prompts the audience to serve as the jury in determining what it means to be a good parent.

Winner! 2010 Premiere Stages Play Festival and the 2010 Jerry Kaufman Award in Playwriting

"Unsettling drama…Ms. Grant doesn't fall into the trap of oversimplifying her characters or seeing only one side of a relationship…this is a sign of Ms. Grant's ingenuity as a playwright."
– *The New York Times*

"Playwright Kathryn Grant is a promising talent with a sharp ear for dialogue…*The Good Counselor* is engrossing, thoughtful and thought-provoking, and worthy of our attention."
–*Talkin' Broadway*

"A searing new play…provides a vivid picture of life's unrelenting hardness, as these people seek small pleasures in their lives, despite their struggles."
– *NJ.com*

OTHER TITLES AVAILABLE FROM SAMUEL FRENCH

MOTHERHOUSE

Victor Lodato

Full Length, Drama / 2m, 2f (Conceived for African-American actors, but casts of other races are possible) / Multiple Sets

The play follows an African-American family in a low-income neighborhood whose lives are ultimately ruined by their surroundings. Clive arrives unexpectedly at the house of his mother and his sister. He says that he is fleeing from the police - but perhaps it's another one of his delusions. Unbeknownst to him, he has shown up on a tragic anniversary. Three years prior, his sister's child was killed in a brutal shooting. As fate seems bent on shattering the walls, mother Mae valiantly attempts to keep house. Mr. Lodato is a 2002-2003 Guggenheim Fellow, as well as the recipient of the 2002 L. Arnold Weissberger Award for Motherhouse

A Note on casting: Motherhouse was conceived for a cast of African-American actors. The author is agreeable to productions with actors of other races; but please note that the play works best if the entire cast is of the same race.

OTHER TITLES AVAILABLE FROM SAMUEL FRENCH

A COOL DIP IN THE BARREN SAHARAN CRICK

Kia Corthron

Drama / 3m, 2f

A Cool Dip offers glimpses into the lives of Abebe, a young Ethopian man with a passion for the unlikely combination of Christianity and ecology, and the family that houses him during his college studies in Maryland. Through their interactions, the play uncompromisingly tackles the issues of drought and social injustice, combining a realistic evocation of human emotion with the fantastical to bring attention to the scarcity of something we so often take for granted: water.

"Half family drama and half sociopolitical exposé, *Cool Dip* makes the socialand ecological issues surrounding water both compelling and fascinating, shedding new light on this most basic of necessities."
– Show Business

"Waxing its most lyrical, whether about activism of the environmental or evangelical varieties, it's one of the most refreshing of the season to date."
–*TalkinBroadway.com*

CPSIA information can be obtained at www.ICGtesting.com
Printed in the USA
LVOW01s1223270713

344945LV00003B/144/P

9 780573 601057